35 FARMYARD FAVORITES TO FOLD IN AN INSTANT
ORIGAMI
FARM

MARI ONO

CICO BOOKS

LONDON NEW YORK

Published in 2013 by CICO Books
An imprint of Ryland Peters & Small Ltd
20–21 Jockey's Fields   519 Broadway, 5th Floor
London WC1R 4BW   New York, NY 10012

www.rylandpeters.com

10 9 8 7 6 5 4 3 2 1

Text © Mari Ono 2013
Design and photography © CICO Books 2013

A CIP catalog record for this book is
available from the Library of Congress
and the British Library.

ISBN: 978 1 78249 048 7

Printed in China

Editor: Robin Gurdon
Designer: Jerry Goldie
Photographer: Geoff Dann
Stylist: Trina Dalziel

For digital editions, visit
www.cicobooks.com/apps.php

CONTENTS

Introduction   4

Basic Techniques   6

SPRING

1 Nestling   10

2 Lamb   14

3 Broccoli   18

4 Flower Basket   22

5 Butterfly   26

6 Chicken   28

7 Asparagus   32

8 Carrot   34

9 Smart Scarecrow   36

SUMMER

10	Sheep	42
11	Sheepdog	46
12	Duck	50
13	Farmhouse	52
14	Snail	54
15	Tomato	58
16	Strawberry	60
17	Bee	64

FALL

18	Rabbit	68
19	Pig	72
20	Tree	76
21	Apple	78
22	Pumpkin	80
23	Corn	84
24	Cherries	86
25	Basket	90
26	Shabby Scarecrow	92
27	Horse	96
28	Green Beans	102

WINTER

29	Barn	106
30	Turnip	108
31	Pheasant	110
32	Snow Rabbit	114
33	Cow	118
34	Boot	122
35	Mushroom	124

Suppliers	127
Index	128
Acknowledgments	128

INTRODUCTION

Origami is the ancient and extraordinary art that creates various shapes from a single sheet of paper. In Japan, origami has become not only a fun activity for children, but also a way of preserving traditional manners and native culture, rather like flower and tea ceremonies do for adults.

In the 21st century, origami has increased in popularity across the globe. This growth in popularity is because origami lets people use their imagination to create anything they can dream up. It is also because origami is an activity that can be enjoyed by anyone, both young and old. At the origami workshops I have held, many participating children were surprised by the techniques and said, "Origami is like magic!" Many parents have realized that, unlike video games, origami can help develop concentration and also give kids a feeling of accomplishment. I have also held classes for high school students as well as adults, and regularly get asked to host repeat workshops by people of all ages. In fact, in Japan origami has been shown to be effective in preventing brain aging and is now used as a physical therapy for the elderly.

In this book, I am introducing a lot of origami vegetables and fruits alongside the really cute farmyard animals. Most of the designs are based on traditional Japanese origami models so once you have mastered these designs you will also have learnt the most ancient techniques and be on the way to becoming an origami master!

In order to make the most of the papers included with this book, first practice the projects with photocopy paper cut into squares, old newspapers, or commercially available origami papers. If you can fold each crease exactly, each finished model then becomes a wonderful thing. Finally, remember to help small children—origami should be enjoyed by together—and ensure that everyone, regardless of age, can enjoy *Farmyard Origami*!

BASIC TECHNIQUES

The most basic skill of *origami* is folding paper precisely and creating strong, straight creases. This can be achieved through concentration and ensuring folded edges and corners match perfectly before firming up creases. To build up models more complicated folds are needed to ensure the paper retains its shape. The four most basic of these are explained here.

INSIDE FOLD

Use this technique to surround one part of the sheet of paper with the rest, enclosing much of the fold between the outer parts of the sheet beneath the fold line.

1 Make a fold, here from corner to corner, and then turn down one corner at the intended final angle below the main crease.

2 Lift the sheet and open out the corner that was folded over then push down the outer point of the edge, reversing the crease.

3 When the sheet is flattened the folded corner will be inside the paper with the reverse of the design showing.

OUTSIDE FOLD

Use this technique to enclose the majority of a sheet with one folded corner, pushing the folded tip over the main crease line.

1 Make a fold across the paper, turning the tip over and beyond the fold line.

2 Open out the sheet and fold the corner of the paper up and backward, reversing the creases.

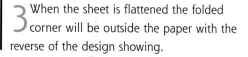

3 When the sheet is flattened the folded corner will be outside the paper with the reverse of the design showing.

SQUARE FOLD

This technique creates a square or diamond shape that can then be used as the basis for any number of *origami* models.

1 Fold the paper from corner to corner then fold the triangle in half again making a right-angled triangle.

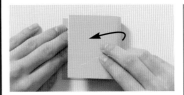

2 Lift the top flap and open it out pushing the folded corner away from you, opening the crease and refolding with two new side folds into a diamond shape.

3 Turn the paper over and lift up the other triangular flap, refolding it in the same way so that you are left with a small square or diamond shape.

TRIANGLE FOLD

In contrast to the square fold, the triangle fold starts with a square shape and converts it into a triangle.

1 Fold the paper from side to side then fold it in half again making a square.

2 Lift the top flap and open it out pushing the folded corner away from you, opening the crease and refolding into a triangle with two new side folds and a horizontal top.

3 Turn the paper over and lift up the other triangular flap, refolding it in the same way so that you are left with a triangle shape.

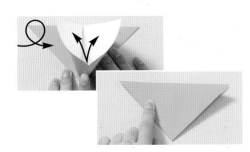

KEY TO ARROWS

FOLD
Fold the part of the paper shown in this direction.

FOLDING DIRECTION
Fold the entire paper over in this direction.

OPEN OUT
Open out and refold the paper over in the direction shown.

CHANGE THE POSITION
Spin the paper 90° in the direction of the arrows.

CHANGE THE POSITION
Spin the paper through 180°.

TURN OVER
Turn the paper over.

MAKE A CREASE
Fold the paper over in the direction of the arrow then open it out again.

SPRING

1 NESTLING

As Spring approaches, the birds that fly around the farm begin to think of building nests and laying eggs. Chicks clamoring for as much food as their parents can provide soon appear. This model is an easy introduction to the origami models that make up the animals of the farmyard so make a simple nestling, or even fill up the nest with two.

SPRING

Difficulty rating: ● ○ ○

You will need:
One sheet of 6 in (15 cm) square paper

1 With the design face down, fold the paper in half through the design to make a crease, then open out and fold the left-hand corners into the center. Fold in the top and bottom edges so that they meet along the center line.

2 Fold in the two right-hand corners so that the edges align along the central crease, then open up the paper and refold the corners inside the model, reversing the direction of the creases.

3 Turn the object over and fold in half along the central crease, then fold the right-hand end over at an angle greater than the vertical to make a crease.

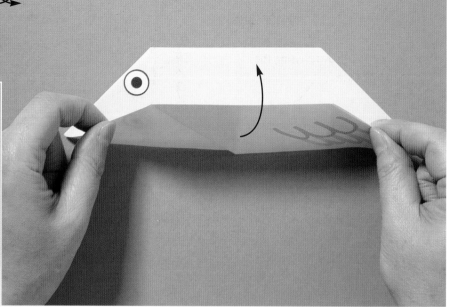

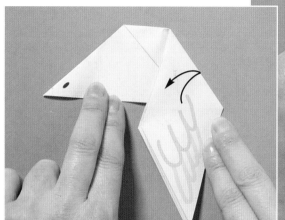

SPRING

4 Open out the paper and close it again, reversing the diagonal crease so that the nose is folded inside the object.

5 Fold over the back of the neck to make a crease, then open out the body and refold the head inside by reversing the direction of the creases.

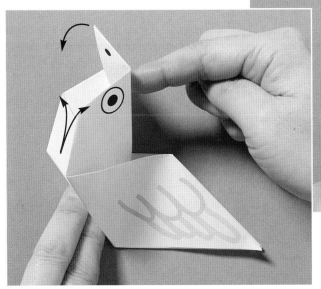

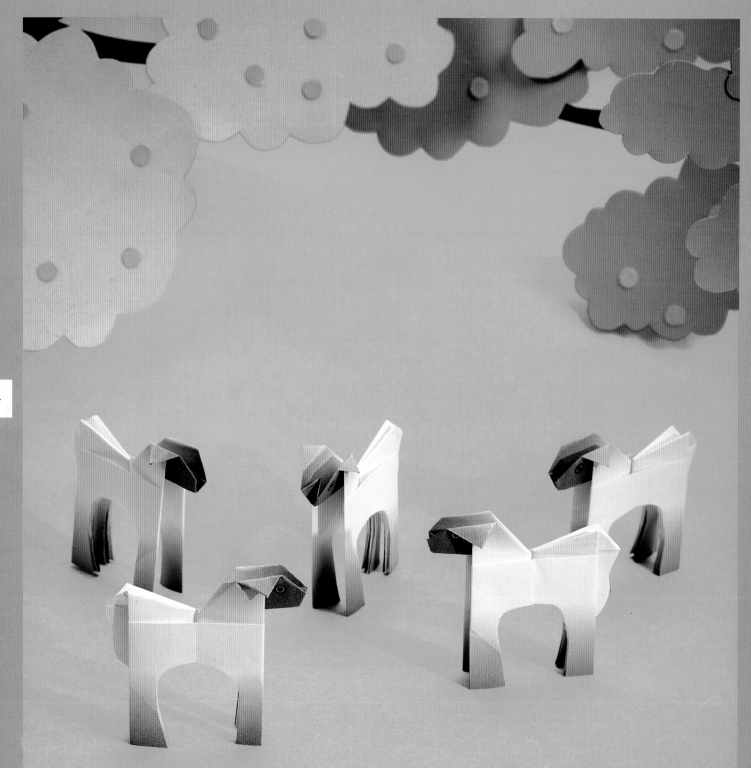

2 LAMB

With the days warming up, the fields begin to fill with tiny lambs running around and playing together in the sunshine. This model can be a little tricky to complete but if you make firm creases at the beginning, the rest of the instructions should not cause a problem. Remember to ask an adult for help when you use the scissors to cut out the shape of the legs and tail.

You will need:
One sheet of 6 in (15 cm) square paper
Scissors

1 Fold in half from corner to corner to make a crease, opening out each time, then fold the corners in to meet in the center. Turn the paper over and fold in half.

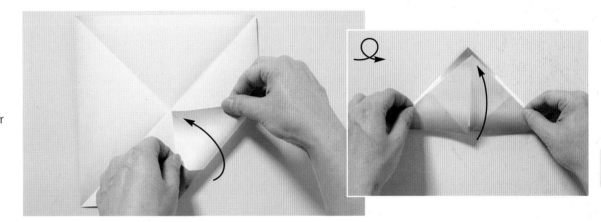

2 Lift the top flap, open it out and press the corner to sit on the top point, making a square fold. Turn over and repeat so you are left with a diamond shape.

3 Fold down the upper part of the top flap to make a crease line between the two outer points.

4 Open out the top flap and press flat into a rectangular shape so that the vertical edges now run horizontally.

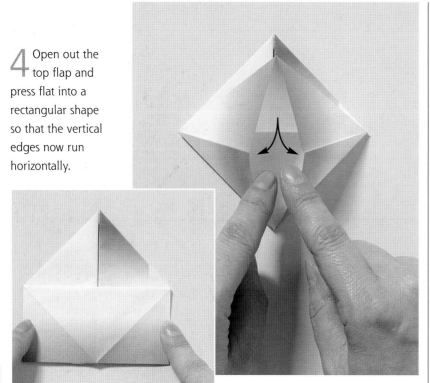

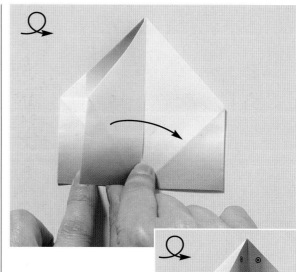

5 Turn the paper over and repeat, then fold the upper flap on the right-hand side to the left. Turn the paper over again and repeat.

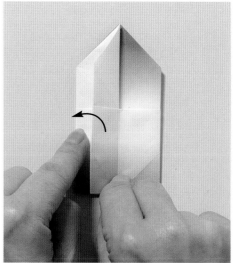

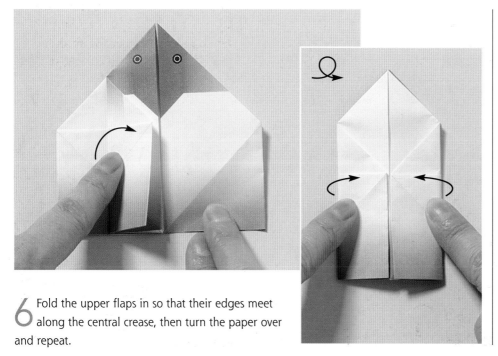

6 Fold the upper flaps in so that their edges meet along the central crease, then turn the paper over and repeat.

7 Fold the right-hand flap to the left, turn the paper over, and repeat.

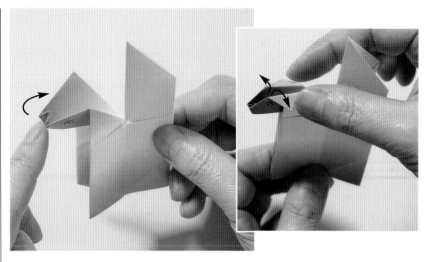

8 Fold over the left-hand point at an angle to make a crease, then open up the left-hand side of the paper and refold the flap inside to form the head.

9 Fold over the tip of the head, then fold it back inside to make the lamb's snout, then fold over the top points to form the ears.

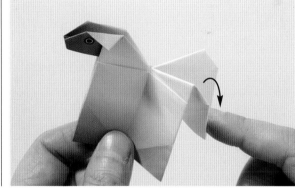

10 Fold over the other point at a greater angle than the head to make a crease, then refold it inside the object to form the tail.

LAMB

11 Use a pair of scissors to cut out the shape of the tail, then cut out the shape of the lamb's legs.

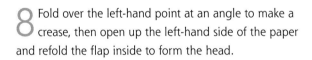

3 BROCCOLI

Although broccoli is not always the most popular vegetable for children to find on their plate, its appearance in the kitchen garden in springtime is another sign that winter is being left behind. To complete this origami model, many of the steps must be repeated four times so be careful to ensure that you don't leave anything out.

You will need:
One sheet of 6 in (15 cm) square paper

1 Fold in half from corner to corner to make a crease and open out. Fold in the other direction, then fold in half again.

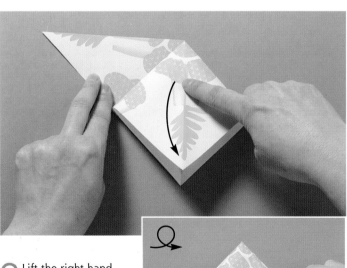

2 Lift the right-hand flap, open and flatten into a square fold. Turn the paper over and repeat.

3 Fold in the lower edges of the side flaps so that they meet along the center line. Then fold the top triangle over the edge of these flaps to make a crease.

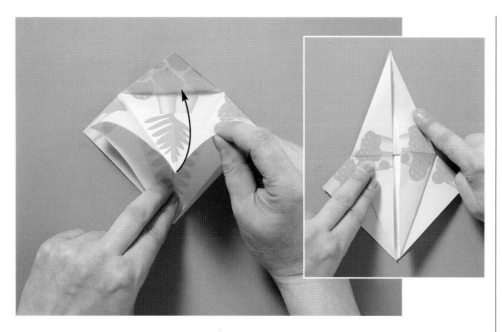

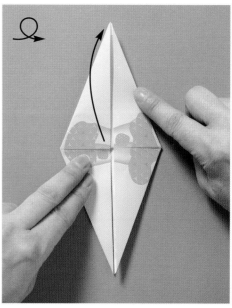

4 Open out the flaps and lift the top layer of paper, then push it away to form a long diamond shape.

5 Turn the paper over and repeat the previous two steps.

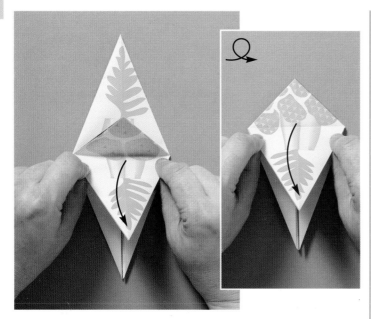

6 Turn down the top flap to the bottom point, then turn the paper over and repeat on the other side.

7 Fold the bottom point back up to the top and press flat, then make two new fold lines between the outer points and the middle of the horizontal crease.

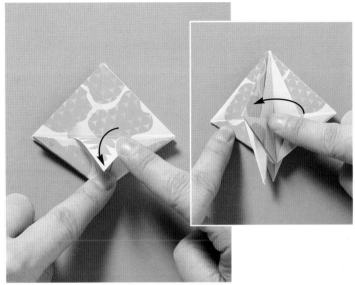

8 Turn the uppermost flap on the right over to the left and repeat the previous step, then continue around the model until all facets of the object are identical.

9 Fold down the narrow point over the edges of the new flaps, then turn the right-hand point over and repeat, again continuing all the way around the object.

11 Push a finger or two inside and form the shape of the vegetable then finish by pulling the leaves away from the main body of the model.

10 Lift up the model and gently begin to open it out.

4 FLOWER BASKET

Picking snowdrops, crocuses, and daffodils while walking around a garden or through fields and woods is one of the joys of Spring. This little basket, which is ideal for carrying a little bunch of origami flowers, is easy to make—just check that the handle is securely held in place on both sides by the folds.

You will need:
Two sheets of 6 in (15 cm) square paper
Scissors

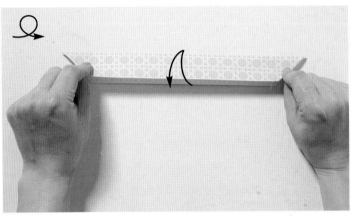

1 Cut the design out of the first sheet of origami. This will make the basket's handle.

2 Turn the paper over, then fold it in half lengthwise to make a crease.

3 Fold the top and bottom edges in so that they meet along the central crease, then fold the handle in half.

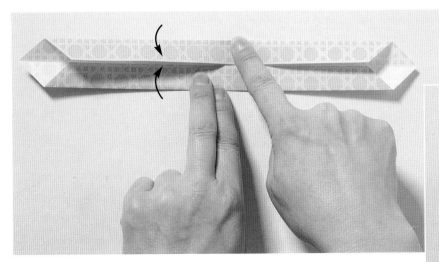

4 Take the second sheet of paper and fold from corner to corner to make a crease. Open out and fold in the other direction, then lift the flap and refold it, flattening the paper into a square fold. Turn the paper over and repeat.

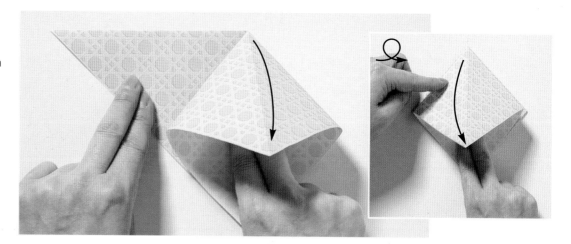

5 Turn the bottom point up to the top, making a fold between the outer points, then turn the tip back down to this fold and make a second crease. Reopen and lay one end of the handle against this crease and close it again.

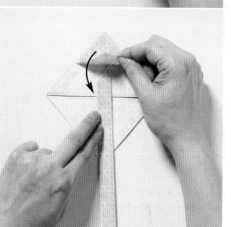

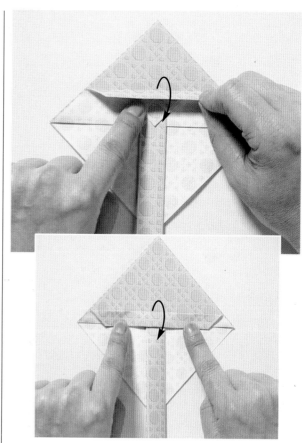

6 Fold the flap over to the horizontal crease twice to secure the end of the handle in place.

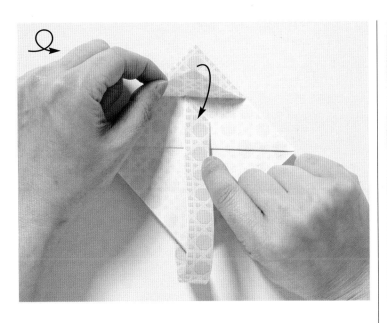

7 Turn the object over and repeat the last step with the other end of the handle.

8 Fold over the outer points to make creases up the sides of the model, then fold all the tips into the gaps on either side. Make sure the folds on both sides of the model are the same length.

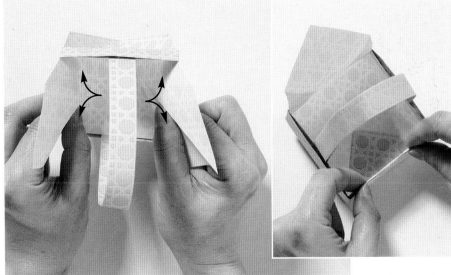

9 Turn over the triangular tip, making a crease across the end of the model.

10 Pick up the paper and gently pry the model open into a square basket shape. Gently tuck in the loose flaps to make the structure solid.

5 BUTTERFLY

Butterflies flit from flower to flower with their prettily patterned wings glistening in the Spring sunshine. This simple origami model can be made in seconds and then hung on a thread from a ceiling or shelf to replicate the gentle beating of the insect's wings. You can even use different papers to make a flight of butterflies that will always fly around your room.

You will need:
One sheet of 6 in (15 cm) square paper
Scissors

1 Fold in half through the design to make a crease, then open the paper out and fold in half again across the design. Use a pair of scissors to cut halfway along the first crease.

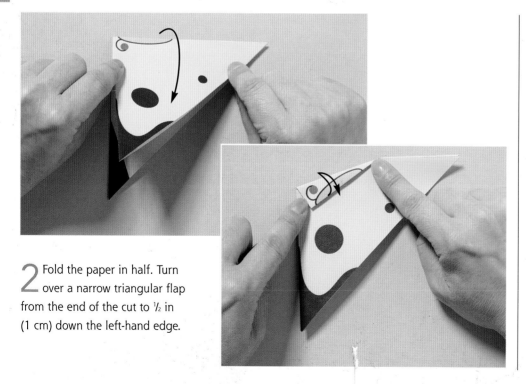

2 Fold the paper in half. Turn over a narrow triangular flap from the end of the cut to ½ in (1 cm) down the left-hand edge.

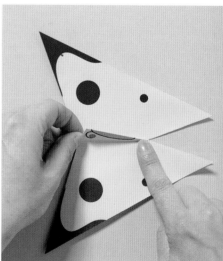

4 Open out the paper using the new fold line as the main crease.

6 CHICKEN

No farmyard would be complete without a chicken striding purposefully across it looking for grain or seeds to peck at. This is a tricky model to make so follow the instructions closely and always check that the pattern you see on your own model matches that shown in the photograph. Remember that the more precise your folds at the beginning, the easier the later steps will be.

You will need:
One sheet of 6 in (15 cm) square paper
Scissors

1 Fold the paper in half through the design to make a crease and open out. Fold in the right-hand edges so that they meet along the crease.

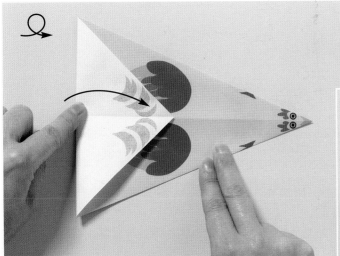

2 Turn the paper over and fold the left-hand end, making a crease between the top and bottom points. Turn the paper back over and fold up the top and bottom points so that the edges align along the central crease.

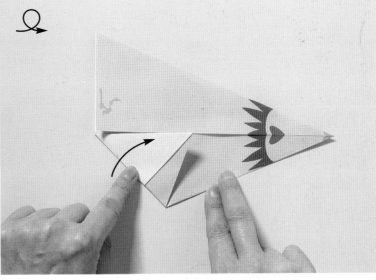

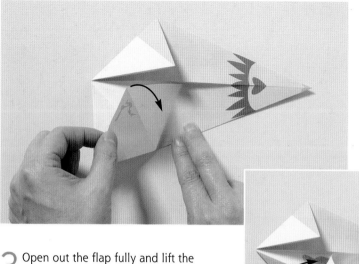

3 Open out the flap fully and lift the corner of the paper, turning it over to the right and reversing the diagonal crease. Refold the flap so that the corner sticks out from the object and the crease of white paper runs along the central crease.

4 Turn back the points sticking out so that their edge runs down the diagonal edge of white paper.

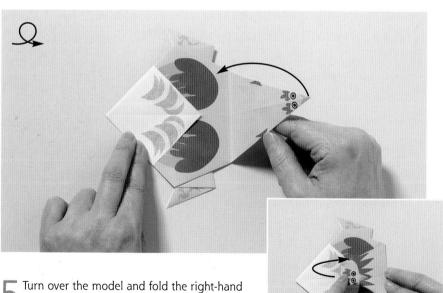

5 Turn over the model and fold the right-hand point over to the left-hand point, making a new vertical fold. Turn back the tip just behind the design for the chicken's face.

6 Pick up the model and fold it in half along the central crease.

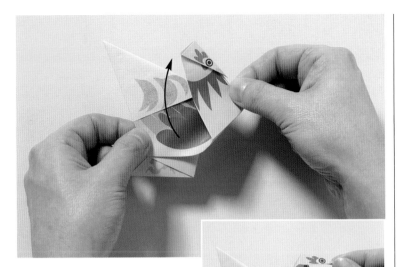

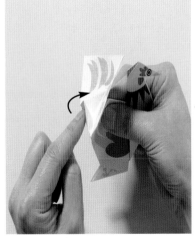

7 Holding the main body of the chicken, pull the neck forward and make new creases. Now lift the head away from the neck in the same way and make new creases. Press flat.

8 Turn over the top point on the left at an angle, then open out the model and refold the tip inside, reversing the direction of the creases.

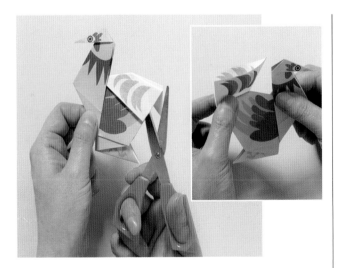

9 Take a pair of scissors and carefully cut up both of the folds of white paper at the back end of the model, then gently reverse the folds so that the design is visible.

10 Carefully open up the tail and fold the end point inside to form the structure of the tail.

7 ASPARAGUS

Asparagus is a delicacy that is expensive to buy but also difficult to grow, so making your own in origami will save you both money and effort! Each sheet can be split in three to make up a serving of the vegetable, so be careful when you cut the paper with the scissors that each piece is exactly the same size.

You will need:
One sheet of 6 in (15 cm) square paper
Scissors

1 Fold the paper in three to divide the design into equal parts, then open out and use a pair of scissors to cut along the two creases.

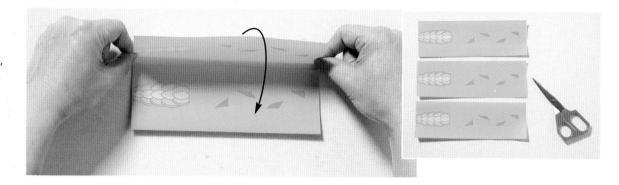

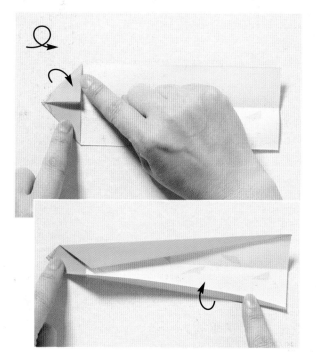

2 Turn over one of the pieces and fold it in half lengthwise to make a crease, then open out and fold over the left-hand corners. Next, fold over the top and bottom edges at an angle to make long, straight fold lines that run from the right-hand corners to halfway along each diagonal crease at the left-hand end of the model.

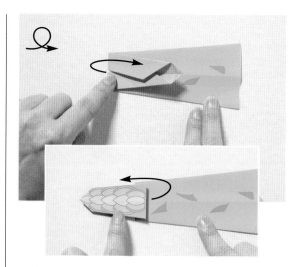

3 Turn the paper over and fold back the narrow end, making the crease one-third of the way along the model. Next turn the tip back, making a concertina fold.

4 Turn the paper over and fold in the two long edges so that they align along the central crease, then fold the two halves together to form a triangular shape.

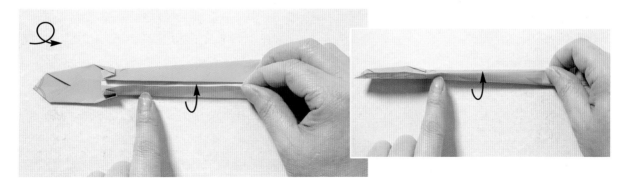

8 CARROT

Unlike asparagus, carrots are easy to grow and every kitchen garden includes a row of them. With their feathery green tops so beloved by rabbits, and rich orange roots, they are delicious and plentiful, so while your mother or father cooks some for your dinner, why not make an origami carrot to grow in your vegetable patch?

You will need:
One sheet of 15 cm (6 in) square paper
Scissors

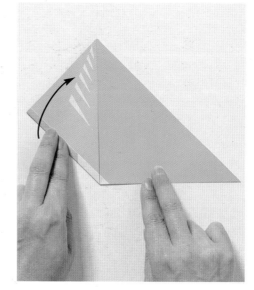

1 Fold the paper in half through the design to make a crease and open out. Fold the paper in half between the other corners, then turn the outer points up to the top corner to form a diamond shape.

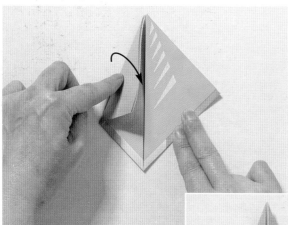

2 Fold over the upper edges of the diamond so that they run together down the center line, then turn up the bottom triangle to make a crease across the bottom of the two flaps.

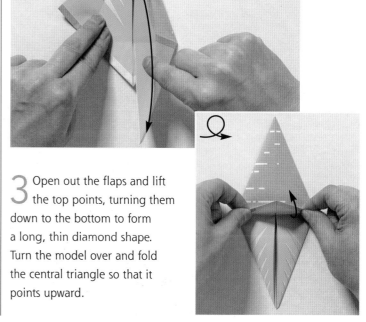

3 Open out the flaps and lift the top points, turning them down to the bottom to form a long, thin diamond shape. Turn the model over and fold the central triangle so that it points upward.

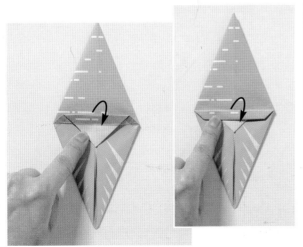

4 Fold down the tip of the triangle, making a new fold line about ¹/₂ in (1 cm) up from the original crease, then fold over again, this time using the original crease.

5 Use a pair of scissors to cut out small triangles from the middle of the model, to form the shape of the carrot's leaves.

9 SMART SCARECROW

A scarecrow is vital for keeping the birds off the fields after the farmer has sown his crops. If the greedy pigeons eat the seed before it starts to grow, his fields will remain brown and lifeless. The more the scarecrow resembles a person, the more successful it will be, and this extremely smartly dressed model will have no trouble keeping the birds off the land.

You will need:
One sheet of 6 in (15 cm) square paper
Scissors

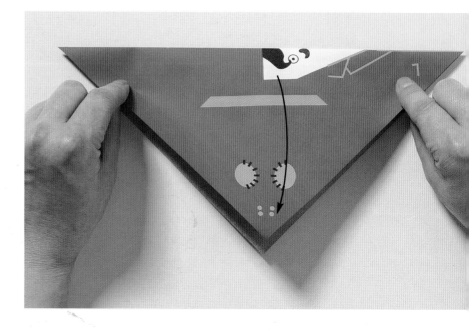

1 Fold the paper in half through the design.

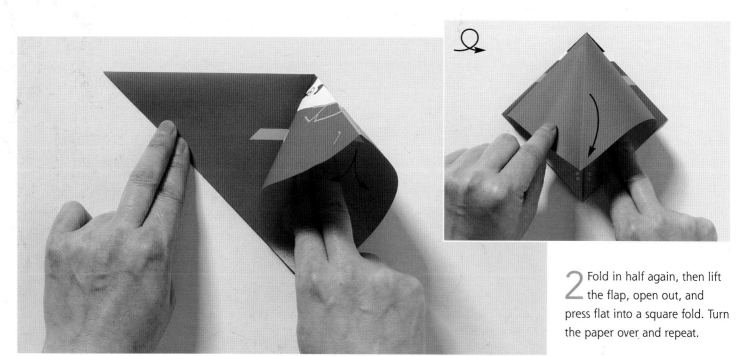

2 Fold in half again, then lift the flap, open out, and press flat into a square fold. Turn the paper over and repeat.

3 Fold the lower edges of the diamond into the center, then turn over the top point to make a crease along the top of the two flaps.

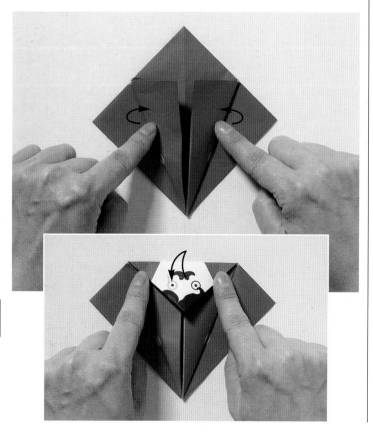

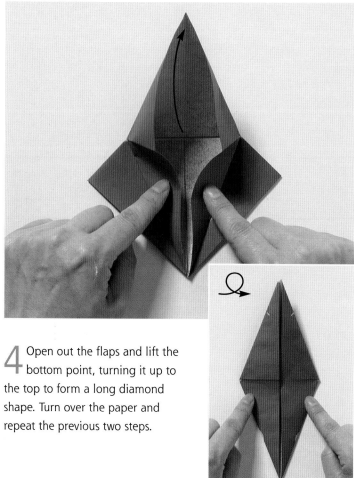

4 Open out the flaps and lift the bottom point, turning it up to the top to form a long diamond shape. Turn over the paper and repeat the previous two steps.

5 Fold up the two bottom points, turning them out to the sides and making diagonal creases. Next, open up each side of the model and refold the flaps inside while reversing the direction of the creases.

6 Lift the object off the table and fold down the main top points using the main horizontal crease.

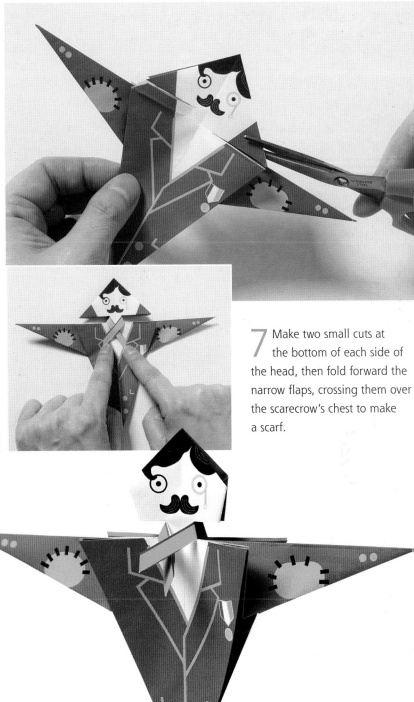

7 Make two small cuts at the bottom of each side of the head, then fold forward the narrow flaps, crossing them over the scarecrow's chest to make a scarf.

8 Fold back the tips on the side of the head so that they are turned inside the gap between the front and back of the head.

SUMMER

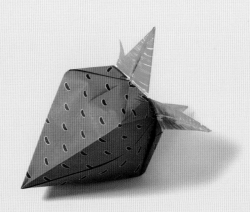

10 SHEEP

As Spring turns to Summer and the days get longer, the animals on the farm spend more and more time out in the fields, and the sheep are enjoying the hotter weather as they look after their lambs. This origami model uses a slightly different type of fold to form the animal's shape so be careful at the start to ensure you finish with a well-formed sheep.

You will need:
One sheet of 6 in (15 cm) square paper

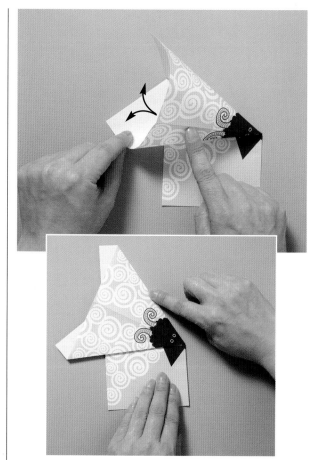

1 Fold the paper in half through the design then turn the top right-hand corner (at the top of the fold) down to the bottom left-hand corner and make a crease.

2 Lift the flap and open it out before folding the paper flat, ensuring that the two halves of the crease in the paper sit on top of each other.

42

SUMMER

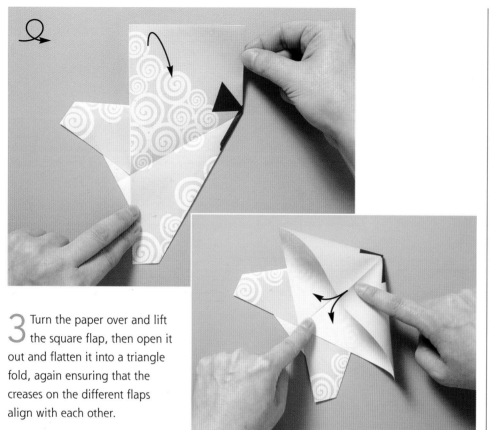

3 Turn the paper over and lift the square flap, then open it out and flatten it into a triangle fold, again ensuring that the creases on the different flaps align with each other.

4 Fold the model in half, checking that the two halves cover each other exactly.

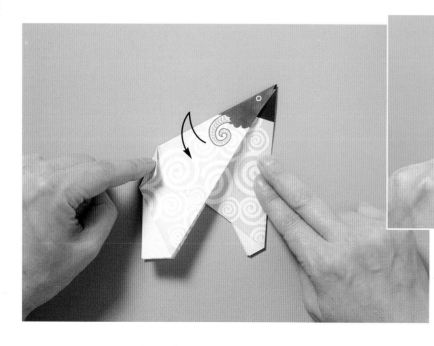

5 Turn over the top left-hand corner at an angle to make a crease, then open up that end of the model and refold the flap inside, reversing the direction of the creases.

6 Turn over the head of the model between the eyes and the horns to make a crease, then open up that end of the model and refold the flap inside, reversing the direction of the creases.

7 Carefully pull the nose forward again, making a concertina fold that will sit inside the body of the model, and flatten.

8 Tuck the loose flaps of paper down each leg in on themselves inside the flaps, then turn over the ends of the legs to make the feet.

11 SHEEPDOG

The sheepdog is the farmer's best friend and closest colleague as he races around the fields to his master's whistled commands, shepherding the sheep as if by magic. This model is actually very similar to that of the lamb so if you practice both, you should have no trouble creating your farmyard of beautiful animals.

You will need:
One sheet of 6 in (15 cm) square paper
Scissors

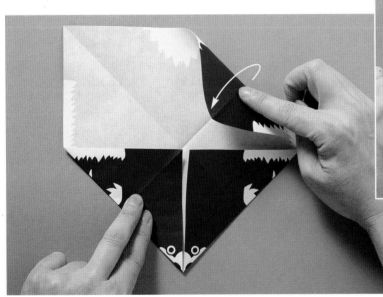

1 Fold in half from corner to corner to make a crease, opening out each time, then fold the corners in to meet in the center. Turn the paper over and fold in half.

2 Lift the top flap, open it out, and press the corner to sit on the top point, making a square fold. Turn over and repeat so you are left with a diamond shape.

3 Fold down the upper part of the top flap to make a crease line between the two outer points.

4 Open out the top flap and press flat into a rectangular shape so that the vertical edges now run horizontally.

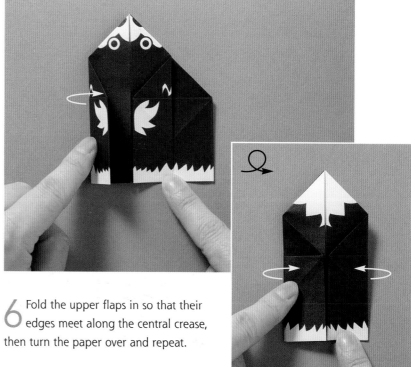

5 Turn the paper over and repeat, then fold the upper flap on the left-hand side to the right. Turn the paper over again and repeat

6 Fold the upper flaps in so that their edges meet along the central crease, then turn the paper over and repeat.

7 Fold the right-hand flap to the left, turn the paper over, and repeat

8 Fold over the left-hand point at an angle to make a crease, then open up the left-hand side of the paper and refold the flap inside to form the head.

9 Use a pair of scissors to cut out the shape of the tail, then cut out the shape of the sheepdog's legs.

12 DUCK

Difficulty rating: ● ○ ○

Every farmyard should have a duck pond where the quacking birds can swim and find food in the water among the reeds and muddy banks. Practice your inside folds so that you can easily make the shapes of the tail, neck, and head on the origami model when required, always remembering to reverse the direction of the existing creases.

You will need:
One sheet of 6 in (15 cm) square paper

1 Fold the paper in half through the design, then fold the two upper edges in so that they meet along the central crease. Next, fold in the bottom two edges in the same way.

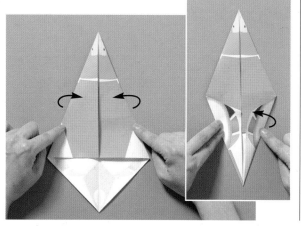

2 Fold the object in half along the central crease.

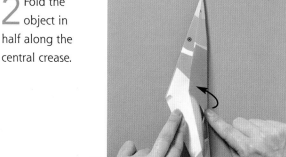

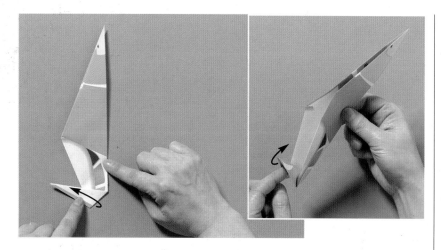

3 Turn over the tail and make a firm crease, then open up that end of the model and refold the tip inside, reversing the direction of the folds.

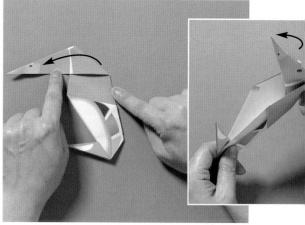

4 Next, turn over the other end to form the neck, making the crease further from the tip and also refold it inside the body.

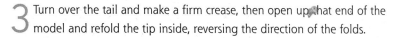

5 Finally, repeat the previous step, making the fold above the eyes to form the beak, once again refolding it inside.

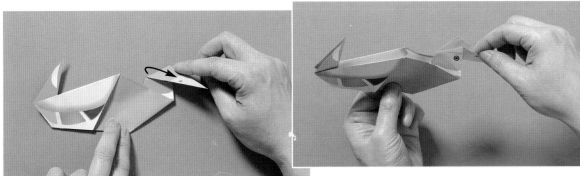

13 FARMHOUSE

At the center of the farmyard is the house and it can often be old or even have a thatched roof like this origami model, which is very simple to make. The most important thing to remember is to stick the two pieces of paper together so that the design of the roof on the back sheet is in the right position when folded forward over the top of the front sheet.

Difficulty rating: ●○○

You will need:
Two sheets of 6 in (15 cm) square paper
Paper glue

1 Stick the two pieces of paper together, using just a thin band of paper glue across the middle of the bottom sheet.

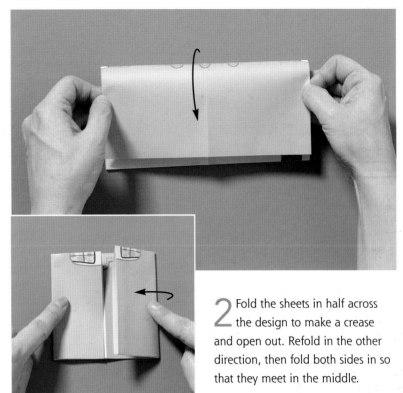

2 Fold the sheets in half across the design to make a crease and open out. Refold in the other direction, then fold both sides in so that they meet in the middle.

3 Open out the two flaps and fold them flat, creating a triangular fold at the top of each side.

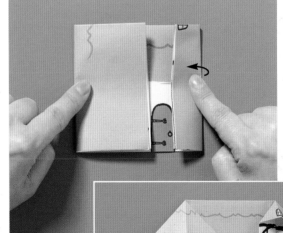

4 To make gables of different sizes, fold the sides in, as in Step 2, but turn them so that their edges lie on either side of the door in the design.

14 SNAIL

The snail is very slow and small but it can ruin a farmer's summer, inflicting its damage by eating the leaves of his vegetables and crops. This little origami model looks the picture of innocence but beware: it will munch away when you're not looking, and there will be even more damage if you make more than one of them!

You will need:
One sheet of 6 in (15 cm) square paper
Scissors

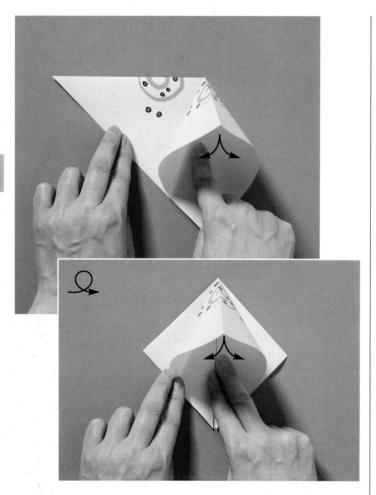

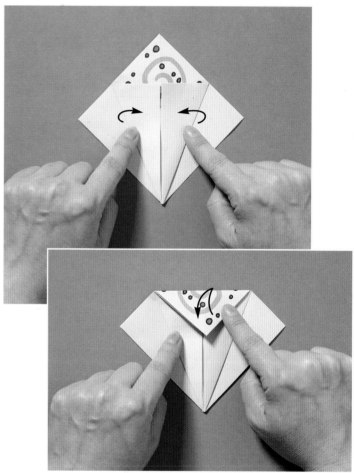

1 Fold the paper from corner to corner across the design, then fold in half again. Lift the flap, open, and press down into a square fold. Turn over and repeat.

2 Fold the lower edges into the center so that they meet along the center line, then fold down the top point over the flaps to make a crease.

SUMMER

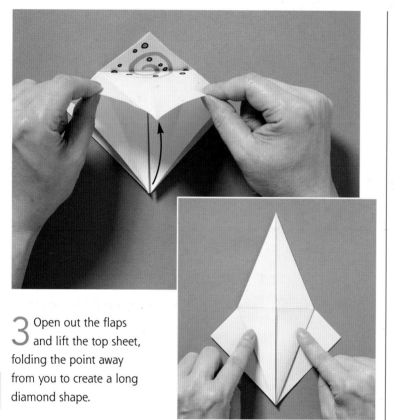

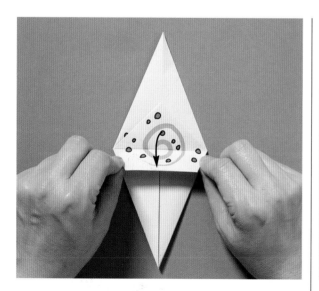

3 Open out the flaps and lift the top sheet, folding the point away from you to create a long diamond shape.

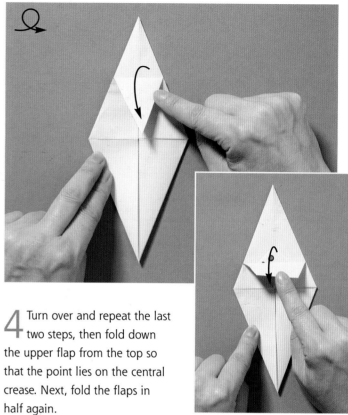

4 Turn over and repeat the last two steps, then fold down the upper flap from the top so that the point lies on the central crease. Next, fold the flaps in half again.

5 Turn the flap over along the central crease to reveal the paper's decoration.

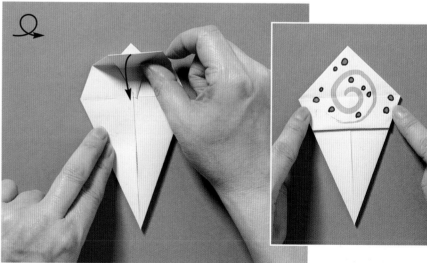

6 Turn the paper over and repeat the previous two steps.

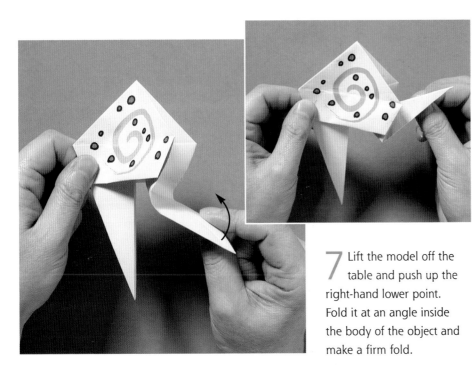

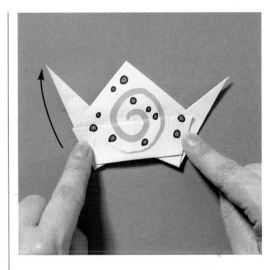

7 Lift the model off the table and push up the right-hand lower point. Fold it at an angle inside the body of the object and make a firm fold.

8 Repeat with the left-hand point, folding this time at a greater angle to finish pointing more upward.

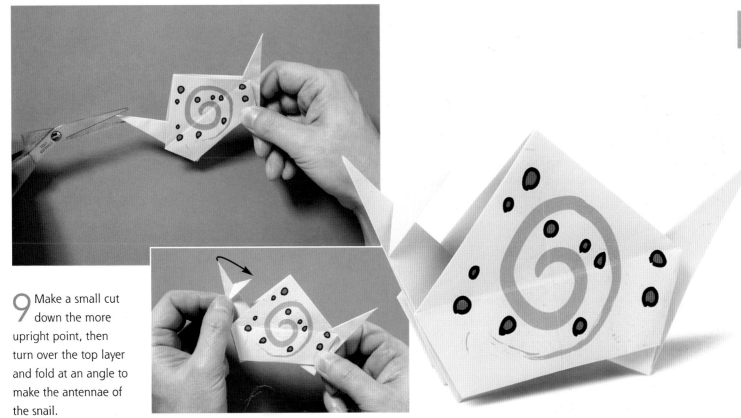

9 Make a small cut down the more upright point, then turn over the top layer and fold at an angle to make the antennae of the snail.

15 TOMATO

There has long been confusion over whether the tomato is a fruit or a vegetable. Whichever it turns out to be, it has long been grown in greenhouses and begins to ripen early in the summer months. This model is simple and quick to make, its clever final folds creating the green stalks that are pulled out when the tomato is eaten.

You will need:
One sheet of 6 in (15 cm) square paper

1 Fold the paper in half through the design, then fold both sides in so that they meet along the center line. Turn up the bottom third of the paper and make a fold.

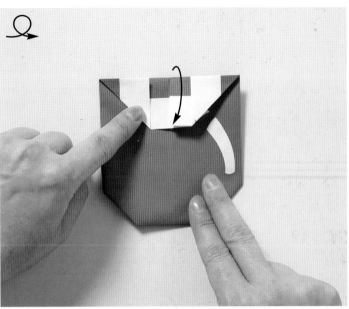

2 Fold up the bottom two corners, about halfway from the edge to the center line, then fold over the top two corners, this time three-quarters of the way to the center line.

3 Turn the paper over and fold back the top edge, using the bottom of the corner flaps as the fold line.

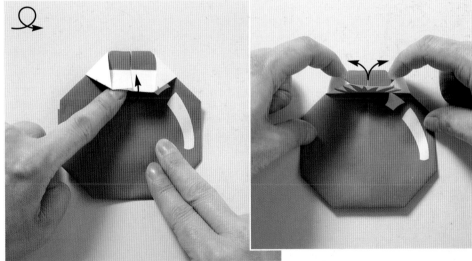

4 Turn the paper back over and fold the top corners over at an angle, leaving a very small gap above the edge of the main horizontal flap.

5 Turn the paper over again and lift up the top flap. Use your fingertips to gently open up the triangular folds on either side and reflatten so the edges run vertically.

16 STRAWBERRY

Strawberries are delicious and refreshing, and perfect to eat on a hot summer afternoon. The cats are not the only ones who want the cream—when fresh, red strawberries are on the table, everyone rushes in to feast on the most famous summer fruit. When you have folded the origami model, finish by using a felt-tip pen to color in the leaves of the strawberry's stalk.

You will need:
One sheet of 6 in (15 cm) square paper
Green felt-tip pen

1 Fold the paper in half from corner to corner, then in half again. Lift the top flap, open it, and refold it flat into a square fold. Turn the paper over and repeat.

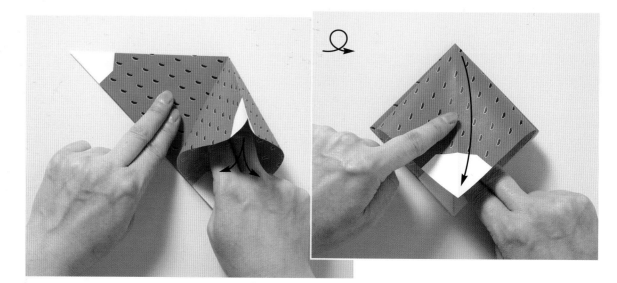

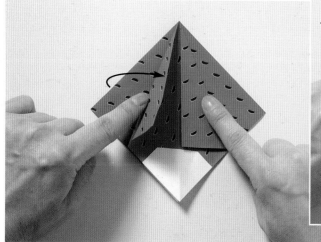

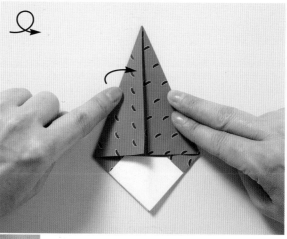

2 Fold in the upper edges of the top layer so that they meet along the central crease, then turn the paper over and repeat.

3 Fold the shorter, lower edges of the top flaps in so that they also meet along the central crease.

4 Lift each flap and carefully open them out by placing a finger between the sheets that make up the flap. As they open up into the new pointed shape, press them flat. Turn the object over and repeat.

5 Turn the top flap on the right-hand side from right to left.

6 Fold in the lower edges of the object so that they meet along the central crease, then turn the paper over and repeat.

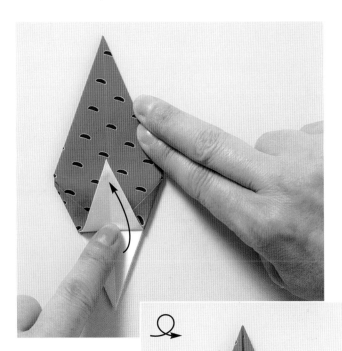

7 Fold up the top layer of the bottom point, using the edges of the flaps as fold lines. Turn the paper over and repeat.

8 Lift the model off the table and gently pry it open by pulling the leaves away from the body. As the model forms, use a fingertip to create the shape of the strawberry.

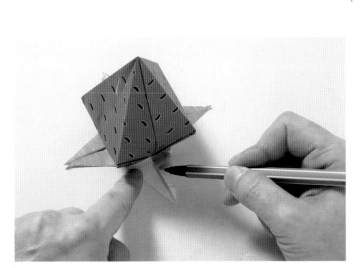

9 Use a green felt-tip pen to color both sides of the leaves to resemble the strawberry when it has been picked from the ground.

17 BEE

The swarms of buzzing bees flying around the farm and yard collect nectar which they take back to their hive to turn into sweet, delicious honey. Like the butterfly, this origami model is extremely simple to make so you can create as many as you like and show them discovering the flowers and plants in your own room.

You will need:
One sheet of 6 in (15 cm) square paper

1 Fold the paper in half from corner to corner across the design, then fold both side points up to the top point.

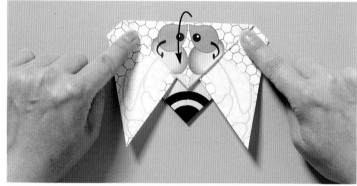

2 Fold the same points back down, making fold lines at an angle from the new side points. Next, turn down the top point making a new fold line just above the side points.

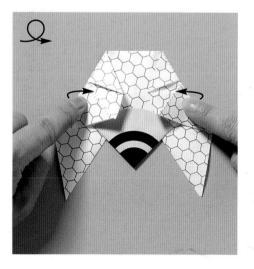

3 Turn the paper over and fold in the side points at an angle, ensuring that they do not touch in the middle and that the new flaps do not cross the edge of the paper.

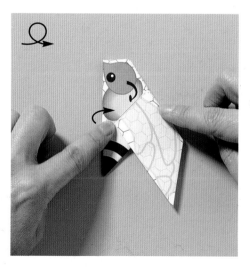

4 Turn the paper back over and fold it in half.

FALL

18 RABBIT

Rabbits playing hide-and-seek in the farmyard are so cute. They come out of their burrows when all is quiet but hide again as soon as anyone appears. This origami model is very similar to the traditional Japanese balloon and also needs to be inflated by blowing in air through a straw. The last step is a little difficult so check no air escapes.

You will need:
One sheet of 6 in (15 cm) square paper
Drinking straw

1 Fold the paper in half through the design then fold in half again.

2 Lift the flap, open it out, and refold it into a triangle. Turn the paper over and repeat on the other side.

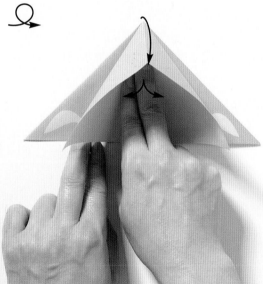

FALL

3 Fold the upper flaps of each side point up to the top point so that the bottom edges align with each other up the central crease.

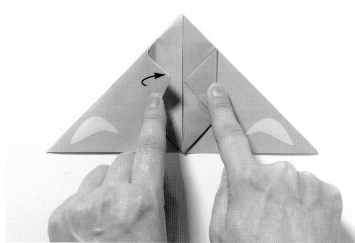

4 Fold the new side points of the same flaps in so that they meet in the middle of the model.

5 Turn over the top points of the same flaps so that the edges align with the folds made in the previous step.

6 Turn the flap made in the previous step over the diagonal edge to make a crease and release. Now lift the side flaps and carefully open up the pocket so that you can feed in the flap just made.

7 Turn the paper over and fold the side points down so that the diagonal edges align down the central crease. Next, turn the bottom points out to the sides, ensuring that the top edges are horizontal.

8 Fold the side points up so that the horizontal bottom edges of the model now align up the central crease.

9 Gently lift the paper off the table and begin to pry it open. Next, use a small straw to blow air inside the model through the hole in its nose until it is completely inflated.

19 PIG

The pigs on the farm begin to grow big when the apples ripen and become red in the Fall. This model of an origami pig is one of the most important in the farmyard using techniques handed down from ancient times in Japan. At the end, if you are worried that the two sides of the pig's back are spreading apart, you can stick them together with paper glue.

You will need:
One sheet of 6 in (15 cm) square paper

1 Fold the paper in half through the design to make a crease, open out, and fold the top and bottom in to meet in the center.

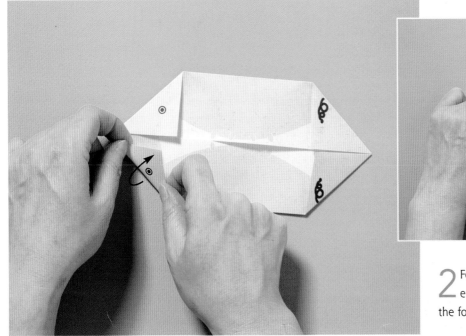

2 Fold all the corners in at an angle, then turn both ends over, using the edges of the triangular flaps as the fold lines, to make vertical creases.

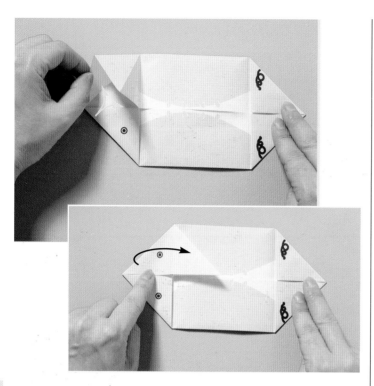

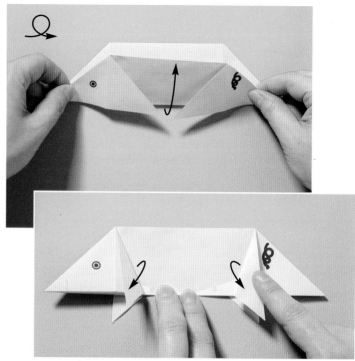

3 Refold the corner flaps into triangular folds by opening up each flap and refolding them into the middle so that each corner of the paper sits on the central crease.

4 Turn the paper over and fold it in half along the central crease, then fold the loose flaps over, making diagonal creases and ensuring that each long edge runs vertically.

5 Start to form the tail by folding up the right-hand point so that the bottom edge runs vertically up the edge of the flap.

6 Lift up the paper and open up the right-hand end, folding the tip inside by reversing the creases.

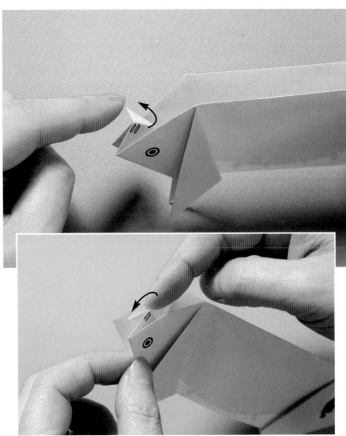

7 Repeat on the left-hand end to form the head, again finishing by turning the tip inside the body.

8 Keeping the object open, turn over the left-hand tip again before folding it back inside the head to form the snout.

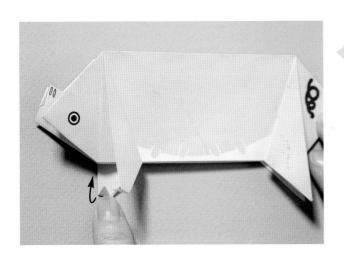

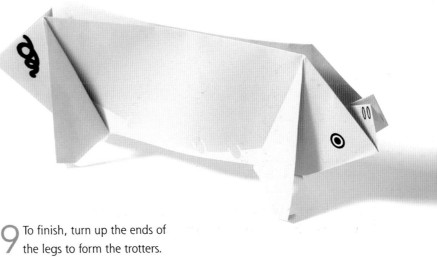

9 To finish, turn up the ends of the legs to form the trotters.

20 TREE

This is the simplest origami model in the whole book so is a great project for first-time folders to try and will only take a few minutes to complete. Just before you finish, after you have joined the leaves and trunk together, remember to remake the central crease through the whole model to allow the tree to stand upright.

Difficulty rating: ● ○ ○

You will need:
Two sheets of 6 in (15 cm) square paper
Scissors
Paper glue

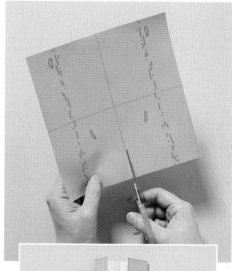

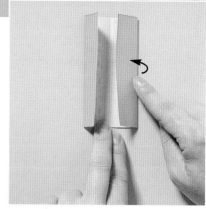

1 Cut along the guide marks of the first sheet, then use one of the quarters to form the tree trunk by folding it in half to make a crease, opening it out again and folding in the sides so that they meet along the central crease.

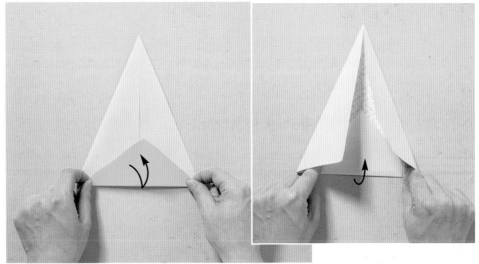

2 Take the second sheet and fold it in half from corner to corner through the design and open out. Fold in the upper edges of the paper so that they meet along the central crease.

3 Fold up the bottom triangle to make a crease and release, then open out the flaps and fold the triangle back up inside the model.

4 Use paper glue to stick the trunk to the main part of the tree and press together firmly. Next, remake the central crease to allow the tree to stand upright.

21 APPLE

The apple is one of the most popular fruits in Japan. Delighting us with their bright colors as they ripen in the Fall, apples hang in their thousands from the trees in orchards across the country. Among them, a large apple called "Fuji" is tinged with pink and is also sweet and juicy. I used this variety as the basis for my own origami apple model.

You will need:
One sheet of 6 in (15 cm) square paper

1 Fold the paper in half from corner to corner through the design to make a crease. Open out and fold the bottom point up the central crease, finishing just above the line of the side points. Next, fold in the side points so that they meet in the middle.

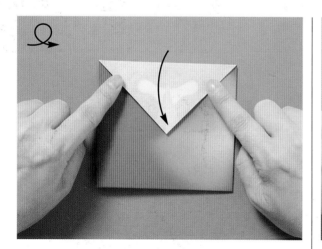

2 Turn the paper over and fold the top point forward between the tops of the vertical edges.

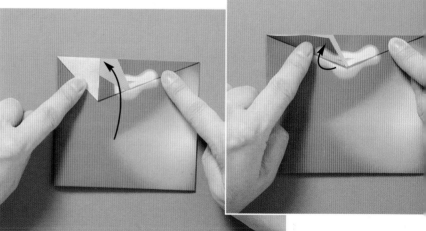

3 Next, fold up the bottom point so that the right-hand diagonal edge runs horizontally along the top of the model, then repeat on the left-hand side.

FALL

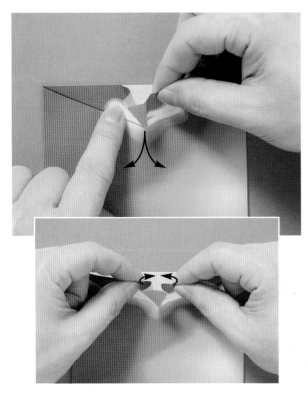

4 Open out these last flaps and refold them so that the corner of the paper comes to the front of the object. Press down so that new folds are created and the corner of the paper sits proud of the square shape of the model.

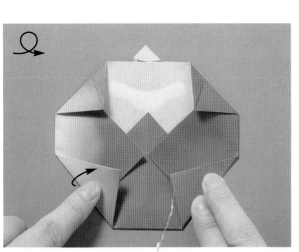

5 Turn the paper over and fold in all four corners, ensuring that the bottom ones are turned in more than those at the top and at a greater angle.

22 PUMPKIN

A pumpkin is often grown by the side of the farmyard in preparation for being the star of Halloween, hollowed out and with a face cut into the side and lit up with a candle. When you make this origami model, always take care when you fold, paying particular attention to the position of the face. If you would like to make your own model of a pumpkin, just use a piece of plain orange paper and draw on your design.

You will need:
One sheet of 6 in (15 cm) square paper

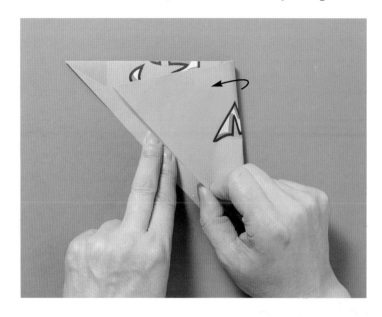

1 Fold the paper in half from corner to corner through the design, then fold it in half again.

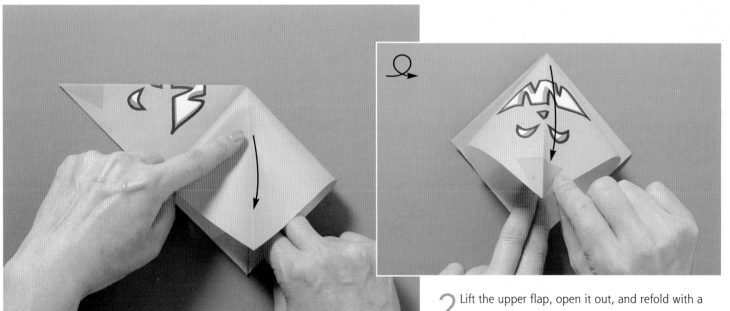

2 Lift the upper flap, open it out, and refold with a square fold, then turn the paper over and repeat.

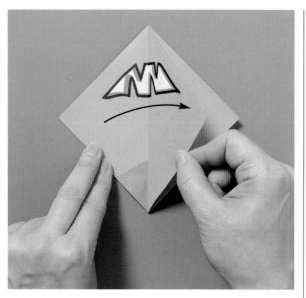

3 Lift the top flap on the left-hand side and turn it over to the right to reveal the design as shown.

4 Fold this same flap into the center so that the lower outer edge now runs down the model's central crease. Next, turn in the upper edge in the same way.

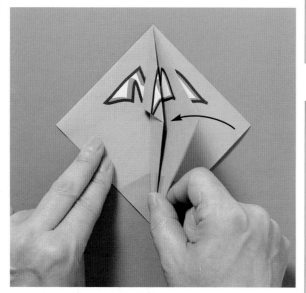

5 Fold both the folded flap and the one behind it over to the left to reveal the same design.

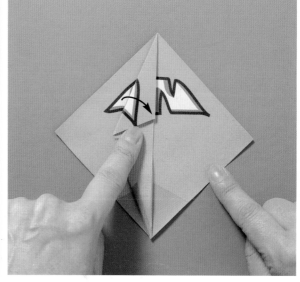

6 Turn in the lower and upper edges in the same way as Step 4, though this time folding from left to right into the center.

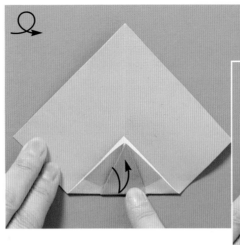

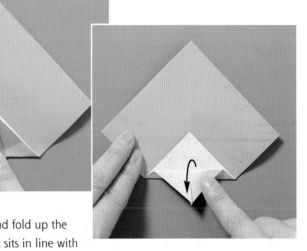

7 Fold the uppermost flap on the left to the right.

8 Turn the paper over and fold up the bottom point so that it sits in line with the two outer points, then turn back the topmost layer of paper, making a new crease just inside the object.

9 To finish, turn over the other three corners to make the finished model into an octagon.

23 CORN

Did you know that corn tastes best and sweetest when freshly picked? Use this origami model to decorate your farmyard, even though you won't actually be able to eat it. Be careful when folding the paper into the shape of a cone—it can be a little bit difficult to get right—but all other parts of the model are easy to complete.

You will need:
One sheet of 6 in (15 cm) square paper

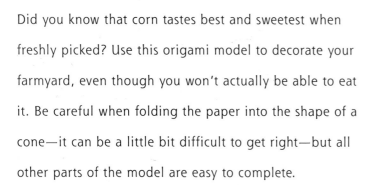

1 Fold the paper in half through the design to make a crease. Open out and fold both edges in so that they meet along the center line.

FALL

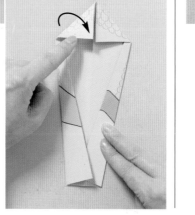

2 Fold in both sides at an angle, making each fold line from the top corner to a quarter of the way across the bottom of the object. Next, turn over the top corners so that the two halves of the top edge meet down the central crease.

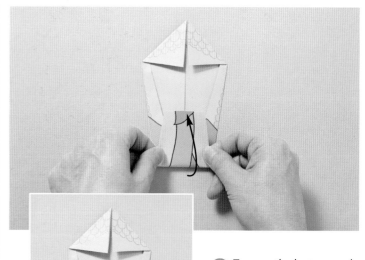

3 Turn up the bottom and make a fold, ensuring the end lies halfway between the new bottom edge and the flaps made in the previous step. Fold the end back, making a small concertina fold.

4 Turn in the sides of the bottom part of the model, carefully creating triangle folds on top of the concertina fold made in the last step.

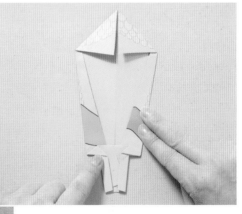

24 CHERRIES

A cherry tree that is in full bloom in the Spring will bear a lot of bright red fruit in the Fall. This is a very pretty origami cherry, and very easy to make, even though the folds are a little unusual. When you place the stem behind the fruit, take care to fix it in the correct position. Make a lot of cherries and they will look very nice in an origami basket.

You will need:
Two sheets of 6 in (15 cm) square paper
Scissors
Paper glue

1 Use the scissors to cut up both sheets of paper along the guidelines indicated on the sheets provided.

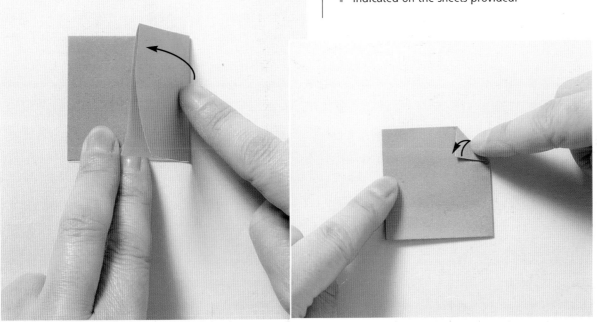

2 Take one of the squares of paper and fold it in half and in half again, then fold over the top right-hand corner to make a crease.

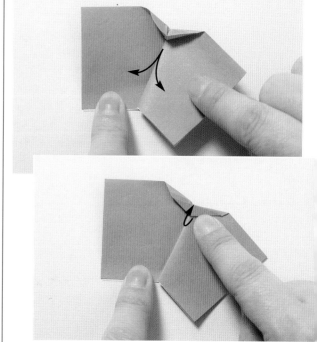

3 Open out the paper and refold the turned corner inside the object, reversing the direction of the creases. Next, fold the bottom right-hand corner over at an angle, making the crease line from just above the bottom of the diagonal edge to about one-third of the way across the bottom of the object.

4 Carefully open up the model and gently flatten the folds around what was the top right-hand corner.

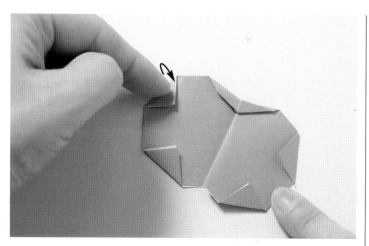

5 Turn over the remaining points to make the model symmetrical.

6 Turn over the object and fold the final corner of paper in behind itself at a similar angle to the previous step.

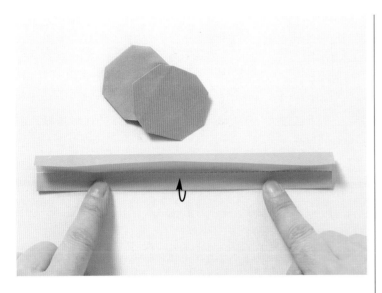

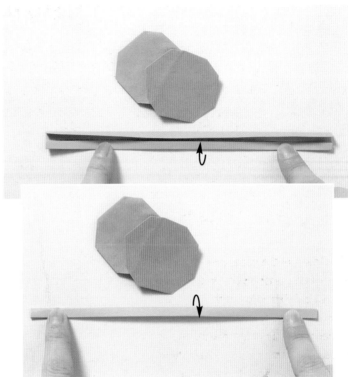

7 Take the second sheet and fold it in half lengthwise to make a crease. Open out and fold the top and bottom edges in so that they meet along the crease.

8 Fold the top and bottom edges in again, then fold the top over using the central crease made earlier.

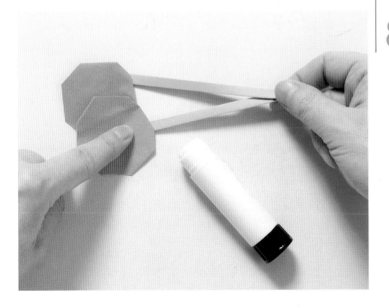

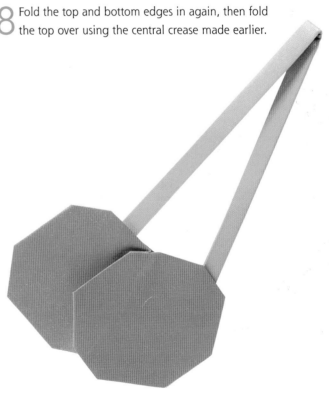

9 Fold the second sheet in half at an angle to make the cherry stem then use paper glue to stick the ends onto the backs of the two fruits made earlier.

25 BASKET

This basket is made from a large sheet of origami paper and is perfect for carrying any of the vegetables and fruits that are featured in this book. It could also have other uses and be made with any size of square paper. Always take care to shape the corners at the finish to ensure the basket has a well-proportioned shape.

Difficulty rating: ● ○ ○

You will need:
One sheet of 9 in (23 cm) square paper

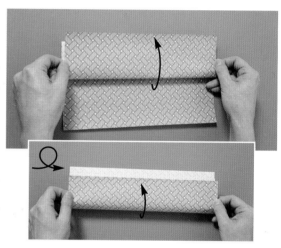

1 Fold the paper in half from top to bottom, then fold the bottom edge back up to the top. Turn the paper over and repeat so that the paper resembles a "W."

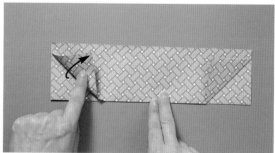

2 Fold up the bottom corners so that the edges now run horizontally but ensure that there is a gap of about ½ in (1 cm) to the top edge of the model.

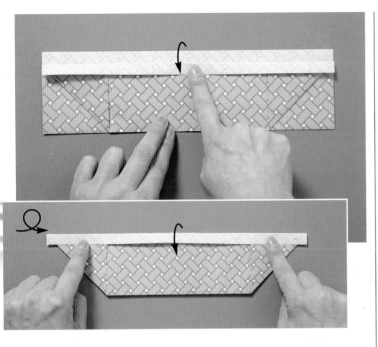

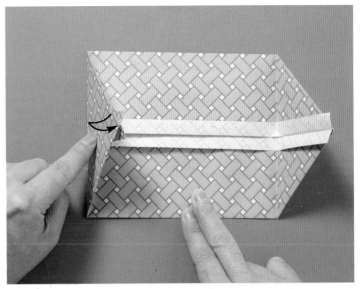

3 Turn the topmost sheet over these new flaps, then turn the object over and repeat the previous step before folding the top sheet over the edges of the new flaps.

4 Open out the model into a lozenge shape and fold the ends over from the bottom of the diagonal edges to create two new vertical creases.

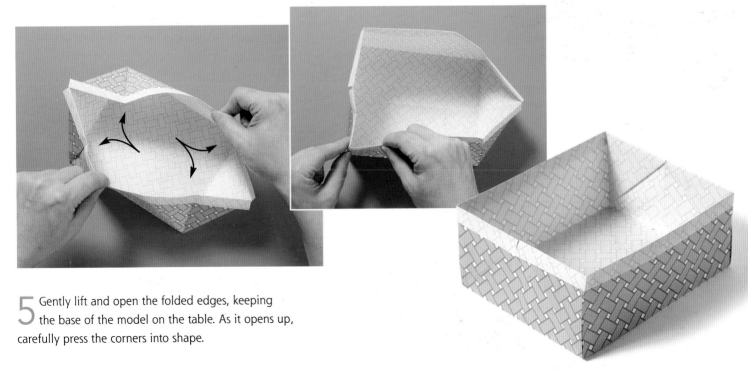

5 Gently lift and open the folded edges, keeping the base of the model on the table. As it opens up, carefully press the corners into shape.

26 SHABBY SCARECROW

The traditional scarecrow was made from straw stuffed inside old clothes, topped by a scruffy hat and propped up on a stake. When compared with the Smart Scarecrow of Spring, which do you think will scare the most birds? To create your origami scarecrow, start by folding the body, then use the scissors to make the cut that will allow you to form the arms and, finally, the head.

You will need:
One sheet of 6 in (15 cm) square paper
Scissors

FALL

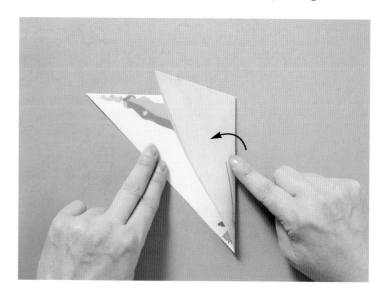

1 Fold the paper in half from corner to corner across the design, then fold it in half again.

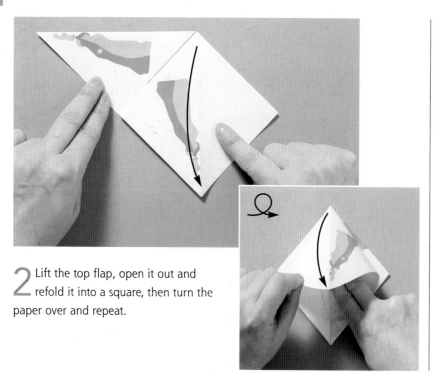

2 Lift the top flap, open it out and refold it into a square, then turn the paper over and repeat.

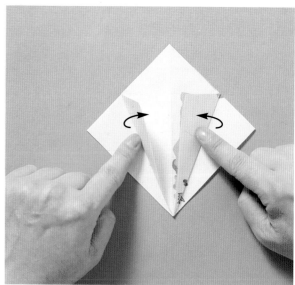

3 Fold in the lower diagonal edges of the top flaps so that they meet along the central crease.

4 Fold down the top triangle to make a horizontal crease. Release, then open out the flaps and push the corner of paper away from you, reversing the creases so that the edges align along the central crease.

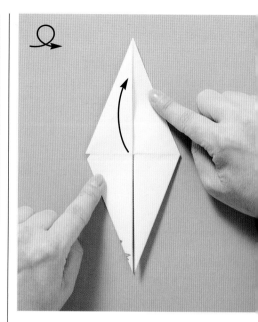

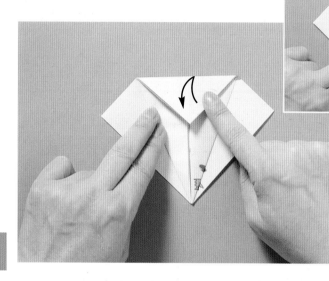

5 Turn the paper over and repeat on the other side so that you are left with the paper in a long diamond shape.

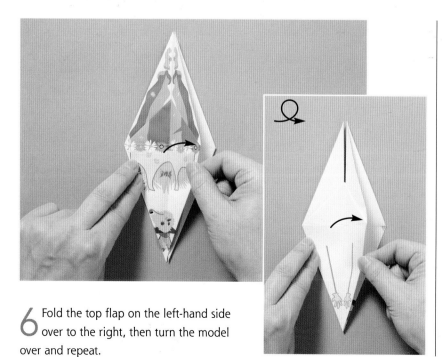

6 Fold the top flap on the left-hand side over to the right, then turn the model over and repeat.

7 Pick up the object and cut down the central crease to just below the line between the two outer points.

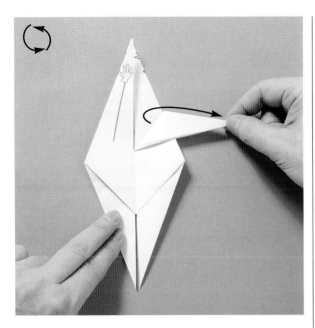

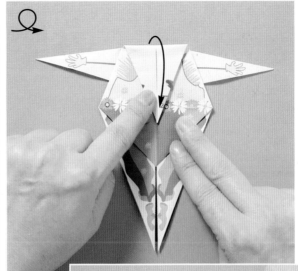

9 Turn the object over and fold the head forward, making a crease line between the tops of the arms. Then fold the head back to make a concertina fold.

8 Spin the model through 180° and turn the top points over so that they point out from the object, but ensure the arms are not exactly horizontal.

10 Turn the model over and gently open out the back of the scarecrow's head, reforming it so that it has vertical edges, and press flat.

27 HORSE

Although it is tricky to make, this origami horse is a delightful model and, when running around its paddock, gives a true feeling of a working farm. Make the body first, taking care when expanding the paper in the middle. Folding the head may also be hard because of the many sheets of paper that lie on top of each other, but do your best.

You will need:
Two sheets of 6 in (15 cm) square paper
Paper glue

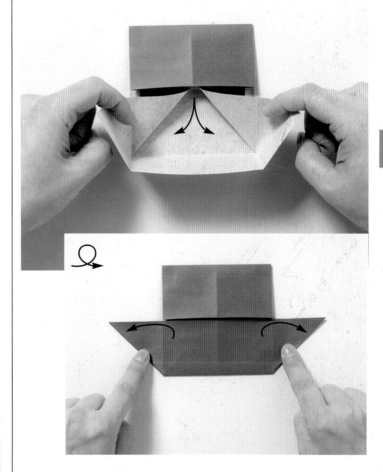

1 Fold the sheet that makes the horse's body in half both ways to make creases, opening it out each time. Turn in the sides so that they meet along the central crease, then turn in both ends so that they also meet.

2 Open out the lower flap and push the corners of paper out from the object, refolding so that they form triangular flaps on either side. Repeat at the top.

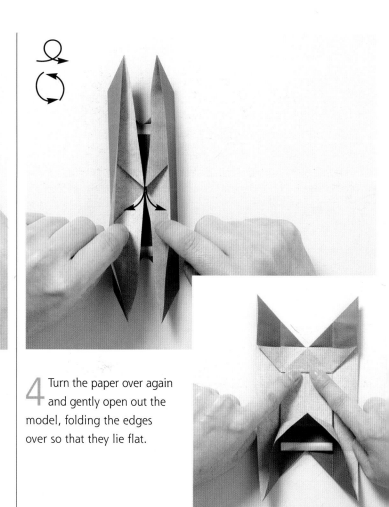

3 Turn the object over and fold the top and bottom over so that they meet along the central crease of the object.

FALL

4 Turn the paper over again and gently open out the model, folding the edges over so that they lie flat.

5 Fold the object in half across itself to form the basic shape of the horse's body.

6 Make new folds on the insides of every leg, creating crease lines from the ends of the legs to the middle of the top edge of the model.

7 Fold over the top left-hand corner of the object, then open up the model and refold the corner inside, reversing the direction of the creases. Put the body aside till later.

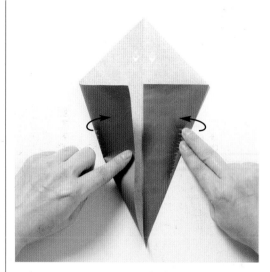

8 Fold the other sheet in half from corner to corner through the design to make a crease, then open it out and fold the lower edges in so that they meet along this central crease.

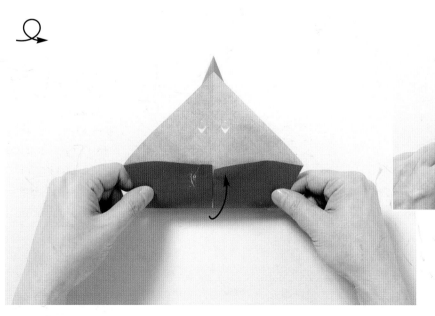

9 Turn the paper over and fold the object in half, then fold in the upper diagonal edges so that they meet along the central crease.

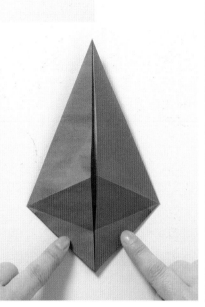

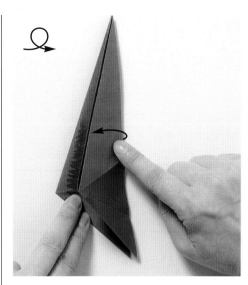

10 Carefully open up these new flaps and refold them so that the diagonal fold is removed and the long edges run down the center. You will end up with a diamond shape.

11 Turn the paper over and fold it in half lengthwise.

12 Fold over the pointed tip at right angles to the main body of the model to make a crease. Release the end, then lift the paper up and carefully refold the outer layer of the creased end, reversing the direction of the folds to make an outside fold.

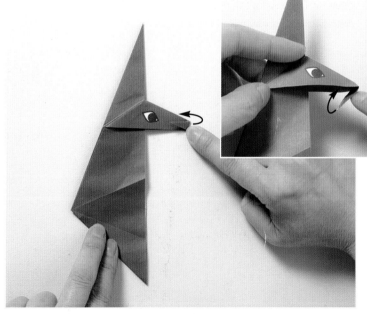

13 Turn back the tip, then refold it inside the head to form the horse's nose using an inside fold.

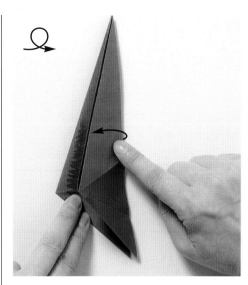

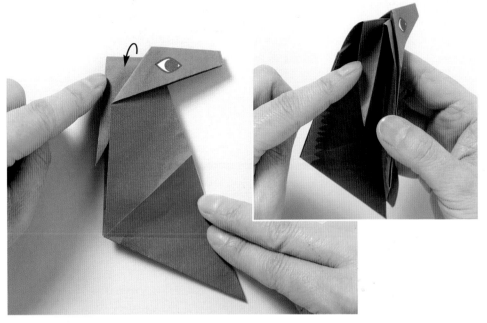

14 Fold down the remaining part of the top point, making a crease inside the neck below the level of the head. Carefully open up the back of the neck and refold it, this time reversing the creases using an inside fold.

15 Fold forward the back of the neck on both sides to reveal the design of the horse's mane.

16 Using a little bit of paper glue, join the two parts together, sliding the neck around the body inside the flaps of the legs.

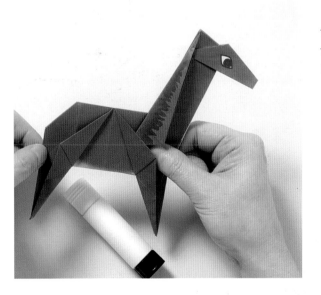

28 GREEN BEANS

Difficulty rating: ● ○ ○

You will need:
One sheet of 6 in (15 cm) square paper

Green beans are indispensable at the table and are also very good for you. This origami pod of green beans is folded in the same way as the Japanese traditional origami boat. Many models can be made into different items—in this case, the trick is to reshape the rounded ends on the bottom.

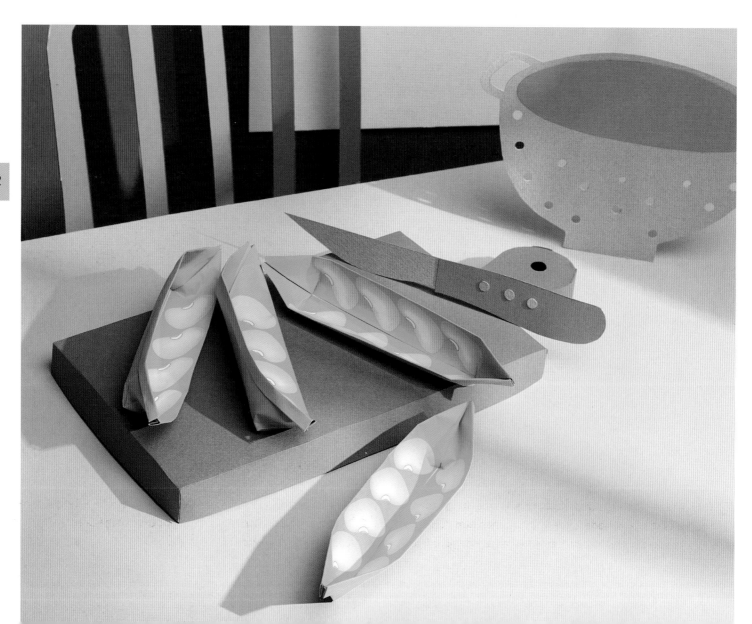

1 Fold the paper in half through the design to make a crease and open out. Fold the bottom and top edges in to meet along the center line, then fold up the bottom half of the object.

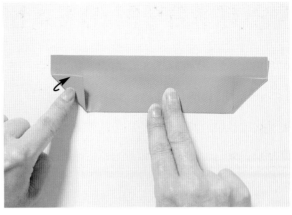

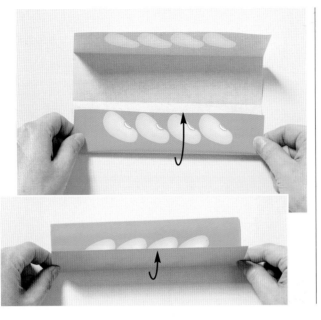

2 Turn over the bottom two corners to create diagonal folds, ensuring that the horizontal top edges of the flaps are about ½ in (1 cm) from the top of the object.

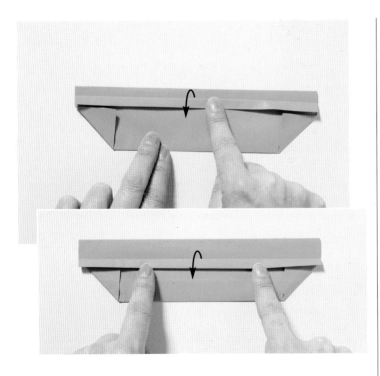

3 Fold over the top edge of the upper flap so that it runs along the top of the flaps made in the last step, then turn over again, making a new fold line along the top of the same triangular flaps.

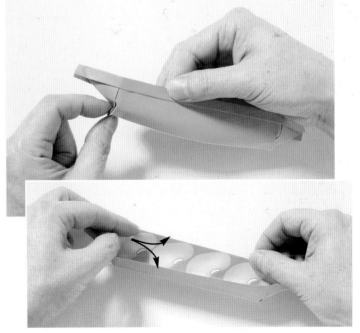

4 Lift up the model and begin to open it, pressing out the bottom of the triangular flaps to form the structure of the bean pod before finishing its shape.

WINTER

29 BARN

A good barn in the farmyard is as indispensable to the farmer as his house. This model stands ready to hold the hay for the animals as well as shelter the cows and sheep in winter. Keep the origami papers clean and easy to fold by sticking them together with only a little bit of glue placed in the center of each sheet.

You will need:
Two sheets of 6 in (15 cm) square paper
Paper glue

WINTER

1 Place the sheet with the roof design face down on the table with the roof at the top. Place a strip of paper glue across the middle of the sheet, then place the other design on top, pressing them together.

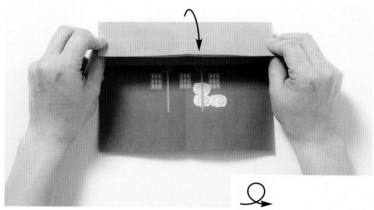

2 When dry, fold the sheets in half both ways to make creases, opening out each time, then fold down the top edge to the central crease. Turn the sheets over and fold the bottom up to the central crease.

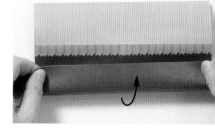

3 Fold in the sides so that they meet in the middle.

4 Lift both flaps and refold, opening out the top into a triangle fold each time before pressing flat.

30 TURNIP

The turnip is a very useful vegetable in winter because it can be stored for longer than any other. This origami model is so quick and simple to make, it will be suitable for children of all ages. The paper provided will allow you to harvest four turnips to make as representatives of winter crops.

You will need:
Two sheets of 6 in (15 cm) square paper
Scissors

1 Cut up both sheets of paper along the guide lines.

2 Take a white square and fold it in half both ways to make creases, opening out each time, then fold the bottom two corners so that the points meet in the center. Next, fold in the top corners, each one about halfway to the central crease.

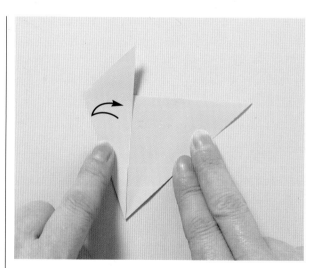

3 Take the second sheet and fold it in half from corner to corner and open out. Fold it in the other direction, then turn both side points to the top, making sure that the diagonal edge runs up the central crease. Open out each time.

4 Carefully turn over the new diagonal creases so that they meet along the center line, making new folds underneath. To finish, add a little bit of paper glue to the end of the green paper and slip it behind the top of the white sheet and press together.

31 PHEASANT

The pheasant, with its beautifully colored feathers and long tail, is often seen striding across the farmyard searching for a bit of grain to eat in the depths of winter. When making the origami model, take care that your creases are strong and clear, as this will allow the reversed folds used in the second half of the project to be made much more easily.

You will need:
One sheet of 6 in (15 cm) square paper
Scissors

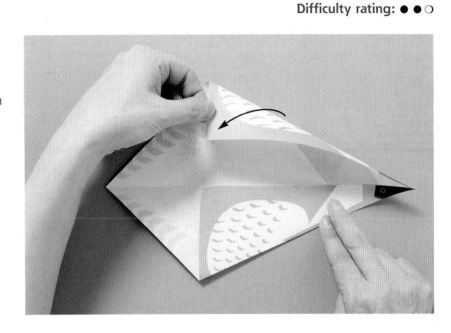

1 Fold the sheet in half through the design to make a crease and open out. Fold the two edges that form the head in so that they meet along the center line.

2 Turn the paper over and fold the left-hand point over to the right-hand point, then turn over the right-hand diagonal edges so that they meet along the center line.

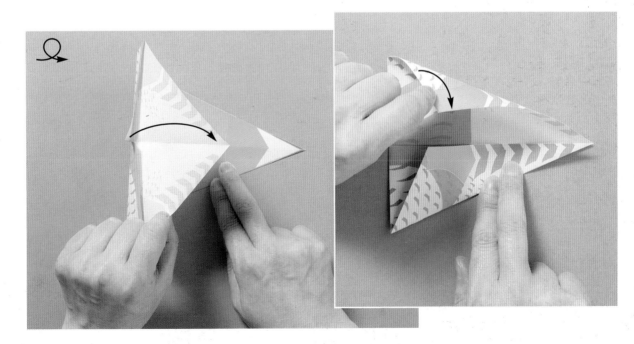

3 Open out these last flaps and refold them to the left, flattening them so that the paper's long edge runs down the center line and beyond.

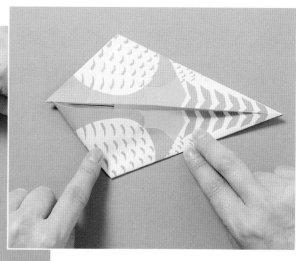

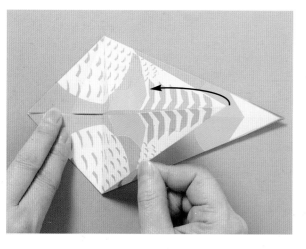

4 Fold the upper flap on the right-hand side over to the left, making a long diamond shape.

5 Fold the paper in half, turning the top of the model downward along its length.

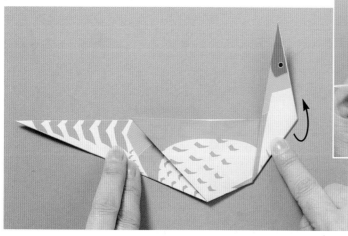

6 Fold up the right-hand end, nearly at a right angle, then lift the model and open it slightly, refolding the tip around the body in an outside fold to form the neck.

7 Repeat the last step by turning over the end of the neck to form the head, then also refold it around the neck in an outside fold.

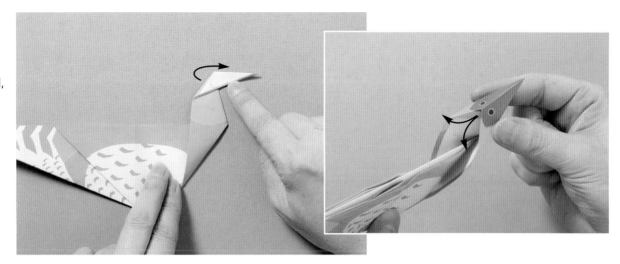

8 Use the scissors to cut through the bottom of the tail at an angle along the line of the design.

9 Fold the new loose flaps in underneath the tail, making fold lines along the bottom of the bold design to the top of the cut made in the last step.

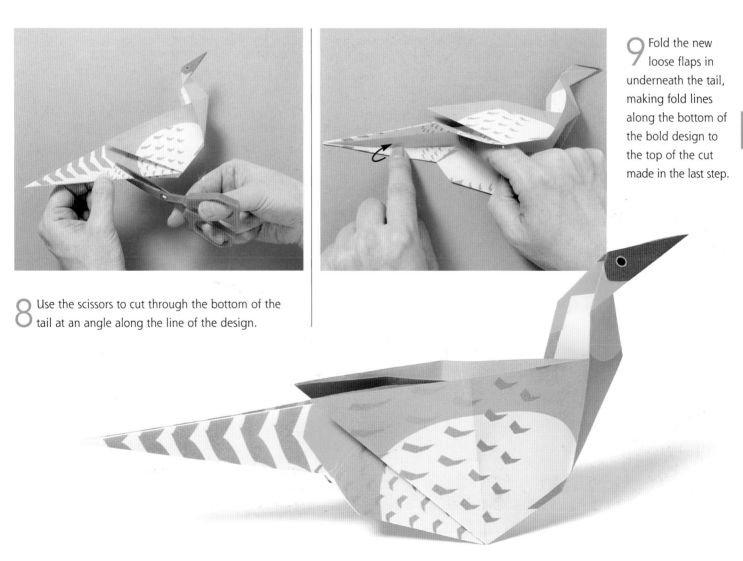

32 SNOW RABBIT

You will need:
One sheet of 6 in (15 cm) square paper
Scissors
Red felt-tip pen

As winter deepens and the cold intensifies, the fur of the "snow rabbit" changes color until it blends into the beautiful pure white snow that is covering the farmyard. All that is visible of these cute little animals as they run and play are their bright red ears. When you put the notch in the ear of the origami model, be careful not to make the cut too long. It is a little difficult, but important for making perfect ears.

1 Fold the sheet in half through the design to make a crease and open out. Fold in the two edges that form the head so that they meet along the center line.

2 Fold back the left-hand point, using the edges of the flaps as the fold line, then fold back the tip in a concertina fold so that it protrudes over the paper's vertical edge.

114

WINTER

3 Fold over the top and bottom corners so that the diagonal creases are at 45° to the vertical edge.

4 Turn the paper over and fold the object in half across its length, then fold in half along its length, ensuring that the colored flap is on the outside.

5 Pull up the colored flap toward the vertical, then press flat around the body, creating new fold lines.

6 Use the scissors to cut down the middle of the colored section of the point to where the color ends.

7 Fold over the top flap, making a horizontal fold line at the end of the cut made in the previous step. Lift and open the flap, refolding it forward so the top edge runs down the edge of the paper below. Turn over and repeat on the other side.

8 Lift the paper off the table and fold back the flaps made in the last step, opening them out into diamond shapes and creating a new fold line between the side points.

9 Use a red felt-tip pen to draw the eyes onto the side of the head.

33 COW

The cow is made by combining two separate origami papers. The body is not as challenging as the pictures make it look, though you must concentrate when making the head and ensure your creases are crisp and firm. If you make more than one cow, you can change the animal's expression by altering the angle of the head or neck fold—have fun trying different ones.

You will need:
Two sheets of 6 in (15 cm) square paper
Paper glue

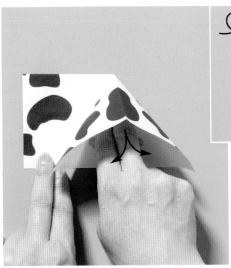

1 Start to make the body by folding the sheet without the eyes in half through the design and then in half again. Next, lift the flap and open it out, refolding it into a triangle. Turn the paper over and repeat.

2 Fold down the top point so that it sits in the middle of the paper and make a firm crease line.

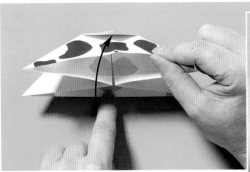

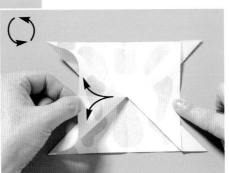

3 Start to open up the paper, folding the top back using the fold line made in the previous step. As the paper comes fully open, flatten the loose flaps into defined triangles.

4 Fold the paper in half down the central crease.

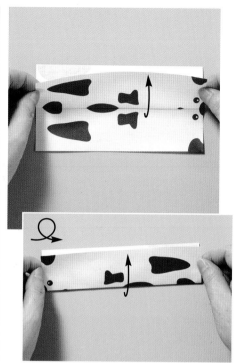

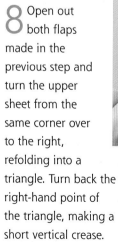

5 Turn over the top right-hand corner to make a crease, then open up the object and refold the corner inside, reversing the direction of the creases.

6 Take the second sheet and fold it in half through the design, then fold the top flap in half. Turn the paper over and repeat on the other side.

7 Fold the upper flap of the bottom left-hand corner up at an angle, making a diagonal crease, then turn the end over the edge of the flap just made to make a crease.

8 Open out both flaps made in the previous step and turn the upper sheet from the same corner over to the right, refolding into a triangle. Turn back the right-hand point of the triangle, making a short vertical crease.

9 Turn the paper over and repeat the previous two steps before folding back the end point, to make a crease, and refolding it inside the object to make the nose.

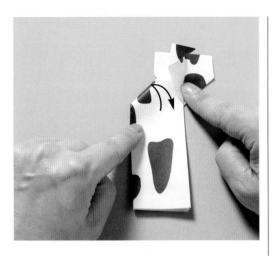

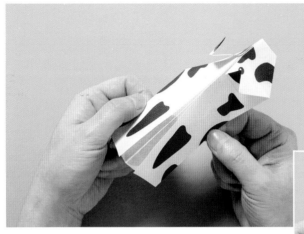

 **10** Fold over the bulk of the paper, making a diagonal crease from the top of the back of the head so that the upper edge of the paper now runs down the back of the ears.

11 Open out the model and then reverse the direction of the central crease while folding the head forward around the rest of the paper in an outside fold, and reversing the directions of the diagonal creases.

12 Fold over the creased bottom corner at an angle, then open the paper and refold it inside, again reversing the direction of the main crease.

13 Take the body made earlier and open it up. Dab a little bit of paper glue on either side of the neck and place it inside the body before pressing it closed.

34 BOOT

Boots are indispensable when working on the farm in winter. Making your own origami boots is easy. The only difficult part of the process is when you are pulling out, shaping, and flattening the toe—and do not forget to pull out the flaps from inside the model to form the heels at the end.

Difficulty rating: ● ○ ○

You will need:
One sheet of 6 in (15 cm) square paper for each boot

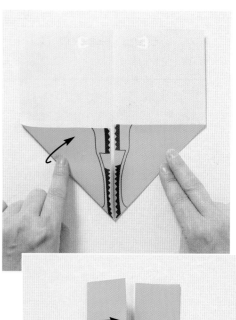

1 Fold the paper in half through the design to make a crease and open out. Fold both bottom corners up so that they meet on the center line, and both sides in so that they also meet.

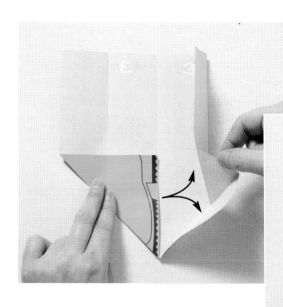

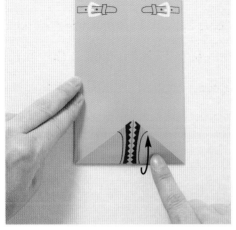

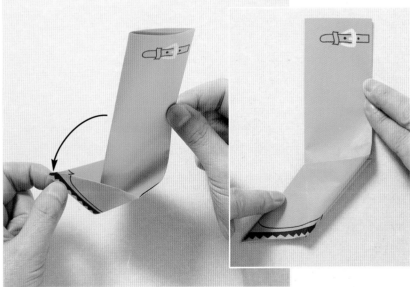

2 Open out the flaps and refold so that the triangular folds now sit on top of the square folds.

3 Turn over the paper and fold up the bottom point, making a new crease line between the bottom corners of the object.

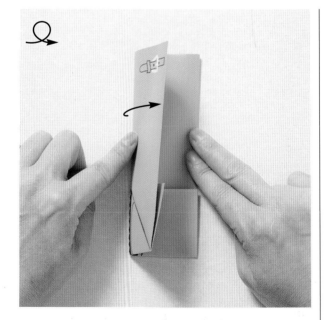

4 Turn the paper back over and fold it in half so that the triangular folds are on the outside.

5 Pull forward the tip of the triangular folds until the diagonal crease runs down in line with the front of the paper. Finally, pull out the loose square flaps from inside the back of the model and press the whole paper flat.

35 MUSHROOM

The design of this mushroom shows the famous shiitake, which is noted worldwide for its delicious aroma. It is so easy to make that even the smallest children will enjoy making it, but don't forget to stick the two parts together with glue at the end of the steps.

You will need:
Two sheets of 6 in (15 cm) square paper
Paper glue

124

WINTER

1 Fold the darker sheet of origami paper in half from corner to corner across the design.

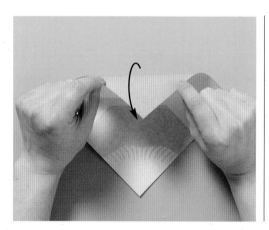

2 Fold both outer points in and down so that they meet at the bottom point and create a diamond shape.

3 Turn up the bottom point to make a crease, ensuring that the folded paper sits inside the darker part of the design.

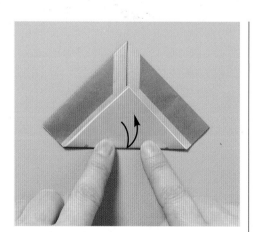

4 Open up all the flaps and refold the bottom triangle inside before reversing the creases on the upper flaps, so that the points are also folded inside.

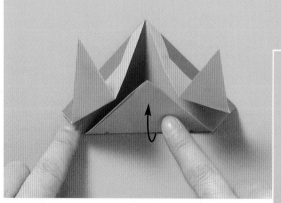

5 Fold over the top point to make a short horizontal edge at the top of the model.

6 Take the second sheet and also fold it from corner to corner across the design, and fold both outer points in and down so that they meet at the bottom point and create a diamond shape.

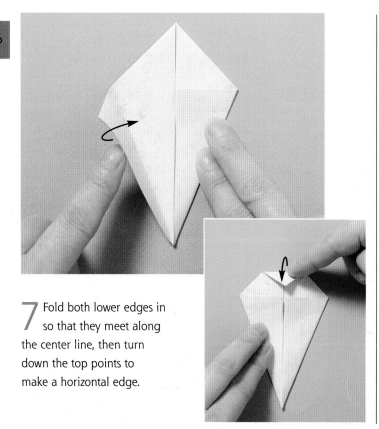

7 Fold both lower edges in so that they meet along the center line, then turn down the top points to make a horizontal edge.

8 To finish, place a little bit of paper glue on both sides of the narrow tip of the second sheet and slide it inside the first sheet, ensuring that the center lines are exactly aligned. Press them together.

SUPPLIERS

Origami paper is available at most good paper stores or online. Try searching online for "origami paper" to find a whole range of stores that sell a wide variety of paper and will send packages directly to your home.

UK
HOBBYCRAFT
Stores nationwide
www.hobbycraft.co.uk
TEL: + 44 (0)1202 596100

MUJI
Stores nationwide
www.muji.eu

JAPAN CENTRE
www.japancentre.com
14–16 Regent St,
London SW1Y 4PH
TEL: 020 3405 1150
enquiry@japancentre.com

THE JAPANESE SHOP (online only)
www.thejapaneseshop.co.uk
TEL: 01423 545020
info@thejapaneseshop.co.uk

USA
A.C. MOORE
Stores nationwide
www.acmoore.com
TEL: 1-888-226-6673

AMAZON
Search for origami paper
www.amazon.com

CRAFTS, ETC.
Online store
www.craftsetc.com
TEL: 1-800-888-0321

eBAY
Search for origami paper
www.ebay.com

HOBBY LOBBY
Stores nationwide
www.hobbylobby.com

JO-ANN FABRIC AND CRAFT STORE
Stores nationwide
www.joann.com
TEL: 1-888-739-4120

MICHAELS STORES
Stores nationwide
www.michaels.com
TEL: 1-800-642-4235

HAKUBUNDO
www.hakubundo.com
1600 Kapiolani Blvd. Suite 121,
Honolulu, HI 96814
TEL: (808) 947-5503
hakubundo@hakubundo.com

FRANCE
CULTURE JAPON S.A.S.
www.boutiqueculturejapon.fr
Store in Maison du la Culture
du Japon
101 Bis. Quai Branly 75015, Paris
TEL: + 33 (0)1 45 79 02 00
culturejpt@wanadoo.fr

USEFUL WEBSITES
ORIGAMI USA
www.origami-usa.org

BRITISH ORIGAMI SOCIETY
www.britishorigami.info

FURTHER READING
The Simple Art of Japanese Papercrafts by Mari Ono (CICO Books)

Origami for Children by Mari Ono and Roshin Ono (CICO Books)

Fly, Origami, Fly by Mari Ono and Roshin Ono (CICO Books)

Wild & Wonderful Origami by Mari Ono and Roshin Ono (CICO Books)

Dinogami by Mari Ono and Hiroaki Takai (CICO Books)

Nihon no Origami Jiten (Dictionary of Japanese Origami) by Makoto Yamaguchi (Natsume K.K.)

ORIGAMI DESIGN CREDITS
Horse (page 96) and Cow (page 118) by Dokuhoutei Nakano

Cherry (page 86) and Turnip (page 108) by Might Project

INDEX

A
apple 78–9
arrows, key to 7
asparagus 32–3

B
barn 106–7
baskets 90–1
    flower 22–5
beans, green 102–3
bee 64–5
birds
    chicken 86–7
    duck 50–1
    nestlings 10–13
    pheasant 110–13
broccoli 18–21
butterfly 26–7

C
carrot 34–5
cherries 86–7
chicken 28–31
corn 84–5
cow 118–21
creases 6–7

D
duck 50–1

F
farmhouse 52–3
flower basket 22–5
folds 6–7
fruit
    apple 78–9
    cherries 86–7
    strawberry 60–3

H
horse 96–101

L
lamb 14–17

M
making folds 6
mushroom 124–6

N
nestlings 10–13

O
opening folds 6

P
pheasant 110–13
pig 72–5
pumpkin 80–3

R
rabbit 68–71
    snow 114–17
reversing folds 7

S
scarecrows
    shabby 92–5
    smart 36–9
sheep 42–5
sheep dog 46–9
snail 54–7
snow rabbit 114–17
strawberry 60–3

T
techniques 6–7
tomato 58–9
tree 76–7
turnip 108–9

W
wellington boot 122–3

128

INDEX

ACKNOWLEDGMENTS

I've been extremely fortunate in that a great many people have helped me with this book, to them I say a very big thank you. As always my editor, Robin Gurdon, has helped me throughout the process of creating the book with his skill and knowledge. I'm also immensely grateful to the photographer Geoff Dann for his excellent pictures. He is so supportive and is always right at the heart of our team.

Friends and family have been tremendously supportive, in particular Takumasa, my husband, who has designed wonderful origami papers for this book. And I also say many thanks to the following: Cindy Richards, Sally Powll, and Pete Jorgensen of CICO Books. And, this book became a very happy book due to the wonderful sensibility of Trina Dalziel, who has designed the background of all the projects. I wish to express my gratitude to her.